CW00375345

Enthusiasms

Enthusiasms

by

MARK GIROUARD

F

FRANCES LINCOLN LIMITED
PUBLISHERS

Frances Lincoln Limited
4 Torriano Mews
Torriano Avenue
London NW5 2RZ

ENTHUSIASMS
Copyright © 2011 Mark Girouard
Edited and designed by Jane Havell Associates
First Frances Lincoln edition 2011

Mark Girouard has asserted his moral right
to be identified as Author of this Work
in accordance with the Copyright, Designs
and Patents Act 1988

All rights reserved. No part of this publication
may be reproduced, stored in a retrieval system
or transmitted, in any form, or by any means,
electronic, mechanical, photocopying, recording
or otherwise, without either prior permission
in writing from the publishers or a licence
permitting restricted copying. In the United
Kingdom such licences are issued by the
Copyright Licensing Agency, Saffron House,
6–10 Kirby Street, London EC1N 8TS

British Library cataloguing-in-publication data
A catalogue record for this book is available
from the British Library

ISBN 978-0-7112-3329-4

Printed and bound in China

2 4 6 8 9 7 5 3 1

CONTENTS

INTRODUCTION

IN THE COURSE of much random reading, in no way connected with my profession as an architectural historian but a relaxation and perhaps escape from it, every now and then I have come across something that has especially intrigued or irritated me: a clue that I want to follow up, a point that others seem to have overlooked, a misidentification that I long to correct, a neglected work that I would like to publicise, and so on. Expanding on these has given me a good deal of entertainment, if occasional frustration, and I hope that reading the results may entertain others. They are designed for pleasure, not instruction, and one of the pleasures for me has been to escape from that burden of a professional historian, the need to provide footnotes and to qualify judgements.

If such literary excursions have been one of my enthusiasms, researching into and writing about my family has been another. I have written a good deal over the years, mostly for family consumption and unlikely to be of much interest to outsiders. But I end the book with three essays perhaps of greater appeal, and with an element of personal feeling in them: about my Solomon ancestors, because they fascinate me; about my grandparents, because their story moves me; and about my great-aunt Evie, as a tribute of gratitude and affection.

Mark Girouard
London, 2011

1

Jane Austen: re-dating *Catherine*

CONSIDERING THE POPULARITY and frequent exposure, not to say over-exposure, of Jane Austen, it is curious that a minor masterpiece by her, although an unfinished one, is so little known, even to lovers of her work. This is her story *Catherine, or the Bower*.

The story is the last of Jane Austen's juvenilia, which she copied into three notebooks in the 1790s. It is much the best of them. In the MS volume it is preceded by a silly dedication in mock heroic style to her sister, but the story which follows is not silly at all. It is the only one in the three volumes that breaks away from the style of a clever, pert schoolgirl, often imitating or sending up contemporary novels and histories, and goes directly for inspiration, as in her novels, to the real people she knew, in the society of clergymen and landed gentry in which she grew up.

Like all Jane Austen's later novels, the opening sentence gets one off to a good start. 'Catherine had the misfortune, as many heroines have had before her, of losing her parents when she was very young, and of being brought up under the care of a maiden aunt, who while she tenderly loved her, watched over her conduct with so scrutinizing a severity, as to make it doubtful to many people, and to Catherine among the rest, whether she loved her or not.'

The aunt, Mrs Percival, is one of the four main characters in what exists of the story. She is well-off, provincial and strait-laced. Catherine is warm and outgoing, ready to flirt with any attractive young man who comes her way. Her aunt sees this as the sign of a bad character and is terrified of her marrying imprudently, or getting into trouble; and so 'though she frequently wished for her niece's sake, that the neighbourhood were larger, and that she had used herself to mix more with it, yet the recollection of there being young men in almost every family in it, always conquered the wish.' Catherine is, accordingly, lonely and bored; she is also resilient and, moreover, whenever unusually depressed, finds she can get consolation in a bower at the end of the garden, which she had built with her two best friends, Cecilia and Mary Wynne, the daughters of the clergyman in the rectory next door. But the rector and his wife had both died, leaving their four children penniless. Cecilia had been sent off to India by rich but uncaring cousins, to be married off to a nabob twice her age 'whose disposition was not amiable, and whose manners were unpleasing'; Mary was living unhappily with other cousins, despised as a poor relation. The sisters do not feature in the story as it exists, but are clearly intended to come into it later on.

Mrs Percival has some distant London cousins, Mr and Mrs Stanley, 'of large fortune and high fashion'. They have two children, Edward and Camilla. She has always put off their proposed visits because Edward was 'a young man of whom she had heard many traits that alarmed her'. But the knowledge that this son is travelling in France encourages her to invite his parents and Camilla to stay. Catherine is delighted and excited. Camilla is the same age as her and she hopes she may take the place of Cecilia and Mary.

She is disappointed: Camilla, freshly emerged from her years of being taught modish accomplishments, is totally and gloriously silly; 'all her ideas were towards the elegance of her appearance, the fashion of her dress, and the admiration she wished them to excite.' Her idiotic prattle much enlivens the story, but drives Catherine mad. Jane Austen, one suspects, grows rather fond of her creation, even though she dismisses her with one of the annihilating sentences well known to readers of her correspondence: 'there had occasionally appeared a something like humour in Camilla, which had inspired her [Catherine] with hopes that she might at least have a natural genius, tho' not an improved one, but these sparklings of wit happened so seldom, and were so ill-supported, that she was at last convinced of their being merely accidental.'

The Wynnes in the rectory had been replaced by the unattractive Dudleys, a family of noble birth but little wealth, unlike the comfortably off Percivals, whose money, however, came from trade. The Dudleys accordingly 'at once despised the Percivals, as people of mean family, and envied them as people of fortune'. Even so, they invite them to the dance that they are giving for their daughter. The two girls are excited in anticipation; but on the morning of the day Catherine develops toothache, and has to retire to bed and give up the ball. 'Mrs Percival grieved more for her toothache than for her disappointment, as she found it would not be possible to prevent her dancing with a *man* if she went.' Anyway, the others go off without her.

Catherine's toothache then starts to improve, and finally disappears. She decides that it is not too late for her to follow the others, and has just finished dressing when there is the sound of wheels on the drive outside, and the maid comes running up to tell her that a young man, 'vastly handsome', has called, and that she has shown him into the parlour. Catherine goes down, mystified, and is not enlightened when the young man embarks on a lively conversation without introducing himself. Trying to work out why on earth he is there, she essays 'Perhaps, Sir, you are acquainted with Mr and Mrs Stanley, and your business may be with *them*.' 'You do me too much honour, Ma'am,' replied he, laughing, 'in supposing me to be acquainted with Mr and Mrs Stanley; I merely know them by sight; very distant relations; only my father and mother. Nothing more I assure you.'

He is of course Edward, returned unexpectedly from France because his favourite hunter has fallen sick. They are both much amused, hit it off together, and go off together to the dance.

And so it comes about that while Mrs Percival is describing to a friend Catherine's disappointment and horrible pain, and how bed is the best place for her:

> the noise of voices on the stairs, and the footman's opening the door as if for the entrance of company, attracted the attention of everybody in the room: and as it was in one of those intervals between the dances when everyone seemed glad to sit down, Mrs Percival had an unfortunate opportunity of seeing her niece whom she had supposed in bed, or amusing herself as the height of gaity with a book, enter the room most elegantly dressed, with a smile on her countenance, and a glow of mingled cheerfulness and confusion on her cheeks, attended by a young man uncommonly handsome . . .

Mrs Percival is astonished and angry; the Dudleys are indignant at Edward's coming without an invitation; the girls present (Camilla included) take offence when Edward leads out Catherine (their social inferior, in their view) to open the next dance. Nothing matters to Catherine; 'her whole attention was occupied by the happiness she enjoyed in dancing with the most elegant young man in the room, and everyone else was equally unregarded.'

The next day or two are occupied by Mrs Percival's attempts to get rid of Edward, and by his flirting with Catherine, if possible in the presence of Mrs Percival, whom he adores to tease. Catherine is thoroughly in love; it is not clear whether Edward 'is any otherwise attached to Miss Percival than as a good-natured lively girl who seemed pleased with him'. In fact, he leaves early one morning without saying goodbye to her. Catherine is upset, but consoled when Camilla tells her that she was the only person that he had seen before he left and that he had asked her to give Catherine his love, 'for you was a nice girl he said, and he only wished it were in his power to be more with you. You were just the girl to suit him, because you were so lively and good-natured and he wished with all his heart that you might not be married before he came back, for there was nothing he liked better than being here.'

The story breaks off soon after, and the reader is left in ignorance as to whether Edward has, as Catherine hopes, 'a heart disposed to love . . . under so much gaity and inattention' or whether he will prove to be the first in Jane Austen's line of prepossessing shits.

Catherine relates in a number of ways to Jane Austen's later novels. It is the first of her stories in which a ball plays an important part, the first to show an awareness of money and social distinctions, the first in which the heroine seems to some extent a self-portrait. It has little in common with the other writings in the three Juvenilia notebooks. Nor does it seem to have anything to do with another early novel by her, unpublished in her lifetime: *Lady Susan*. This is written in letter form and is usually dated 1794. It is a short, competently told story of an unscrupulous woman, suggestive of a reading of *Les Liaisons Dangereuses*. It could have been written by someone else; there is no sound of that distinctive voice, already apparent in *Catherine*.

So what is the date of *Catherine*? The juvenilia appear to have been written in 1787–93. The dedication that precedes

Catherine is dated August 1792, and the unfinished novel has always been dated accordingly. R. W. Chapman, the great Austen expert, accepts that date but comments that the fragment 'is unique among these juvenile effusions; in spite of the absurd dedication, this is Jane Austen's first essay in serious fiction.'

The dedication, to her sister Cassandra, runs as follows:

Madam

Encouraged by your warm patronage of the beautiful Cassandra and the History of England, which through your generous support have obtained a place in every library in the Kingdom, and run through threescore editions, I take the liberty of begging the same exertions in favour of the following novel, which I humbly flatter myself, possesses merit beyond any already published, or any that will ever in future appear, except such as may proceed from the pen of Your Most Grateful Humble Servant.

The clash between dedication and story, and between the story and the rest of the juvenilia, and the fact that the numerous other dedications in the juvenilia always mention it if they precede an unfinished work, make it tempting to go one step further than Chapman, disassociate dedication and story entirely, and suggest that Jane Austen wrote out the dedication for a story that she did not subsequently copy in; and that instead she used the blank pages at some later date, to copy in *Catherine*.

If one accepts that *Catherine* does *not* date from 1792, and looks for another and later date to assign it to, one comes across a passage in Jane Austen's earliest surviving letter, written to her sister on 10 January 1796, and describing a ball of the previous evening. 'You scold me so much in the nice long letter which I have this moment received from you, that I am almost afraid to tell you how my Irish friend and I behaved. Imagine to yourself everything most profligate and shocking in the way of dancing and sitting down together. . . I can expose myself only once more, because he leaves the country soon, after next Friday. He is a very gentlemanlike, good-looking, pleasant young man, I assure you.'

'My Irish friend' was Tom Lefroy, the Irish nephew of the Lefroys who lived at Ashe rectory, a few miles from the Austens' Steventon. Jane Austen had danced with him at two previous balls, and in her next letter, on 15 January, she writes: 'At length the day is come on which I am to flirt my last with Tom Lefroy, and when you receive this it will be over – My tears flow as I write, at the melancholy idea.'

'Profligate' and 'shocking' are adjectives much used in *Catherine*, but not in the other juvenilia. Jane Austen's report of her behaviour with her young man at the ball is suggestive of Catherine's behaviour with Edward Stanley. Her flirtation with Tom Lefroy, as described years later by Jane Austen's sister-in-law to her daughter, is equally suggestive of Catherine and Stanley: 'It was a disappointment' but Tom's aunt, Mrs Lefroy, 'sent the gentleman off at the end of a *very* few weeks, that no more mischief might be done . . . There was *no* engagement and never *had* been . . . Nothing to call ill usage, and no very serious sorrow endured.' On the other hand, cousins of Tom, who disliked him, thought that he had behaved badly. Lefroy himself, as an old man talking to his nephew, 'said in so many words that he was in love with her, although he qualified his confession by saying it was a boyish love'.

These were all reminiscences given many decades later. The only contemporary references that have come to light are three in Jane Austen's letters. Two have already been quoted. Then comes a gap of seven months, in which she wrote at least one letter, among those which her sister Cassandra destroyed. The surviving letters then resume, with no reference to Tom Lefroy, until in November 1798 she reports visiting Mrs Lefroy and how 'of her nephew she said nothing at all, and of her friend very little. She did not once mention the name of the former to *me*, and I was too proud to make enquiries; but on my father afterwards asking where he was, I learnt that he had gone back to London in his way to Ireland, where he is called to the Bar and means to practise.' (He was to end up, at the end of his long life, as Chief Justice of Ireland.) He had, it appeared, been staying with his aunt, but had not bothered to come and see the Austens. Her sentence 'I was too proud' seems to reveal that her feelings had been more seriously engaged than the playful tone of her first two letters would suggest – just how seriously will probably never be known.

The thesis of this essay is that *Catherine* was written in the winter of 1795–6, that it was started with gaiety in the heat of her relationship with Tom Lefroy, and that it was broken off when the relationship came to nothing. This dating would place it after *Susan* and the first version of *Sense and Sensibility*, written in letter form, and before the first version of *Pride and Prejudice*.

The history of Jane Austen's first three novels is curious and confusing. All of them germinated over many years before they were published. The future *Pride and Prejudice* was written as *First Impressions* in 1796, and offered to a publisher in 1797, but refused unread. The future *Sense and Sensibility*, having been written in letter-form as *Elinor and Marianne* in 1795, was rewritten in narrative form as *Sense and Sensibility* in 1797. The future *Northanger Abbey* was written as *Susan* in 1798, was revised in 1803, offered to a publisher and accepted. But it sat in the publisher's office unpublished for thirteen years. Finally, *Sense and Sensibility* was accepted by a publisher in 1810. It came out in 1811 and was the first book by Jane Austen to be published. Its success led to the conversion of *First Impressions* into *Pride and Prejudice* and its publication in 1813. *Susan* was bought back from the original publisher in 1816, and brought out, by a different one, as *Northanger Abbey* in 1818, after Jane Austen's death.

By the time of their final publication all three novels had certainly been revised and altered, it is probable considerably, but there is no means of telling how much, because none of the earlier versions have come to light.

If this redating of *Catherine* is correct it becomes, apart from its own value as a story, of interest as giving an idea of what *Pride and Prejudice* might have been like in its original version as *First Impressions*, written, according to this theory, immediately after *Catherine*. R. W. Chapman says of Jane Austen that 'she polished and polished till the finished surface of her fiction had a brilliance which delighted her admirers, but also an apparent hardness which has concealed from many readers the flow of imagination which lies beneath it.' But he thought, and one can agree with him, that *Pride and Prejudice*, above all her books, retained a youthful exuberance showing through the polish. In *Catherine* one gets the youthful exuberance unrefined.

Amongst other changes, Jane Austen's drafts must have needed alterations to bring them in line with growing early nineteenth-century notions of propriety. One can see a modest beginning of this in *Catherine* – at some stage the original title was in fact altered from *Kitty, or the Bower*, and the name of the heroine changed in most places in the text from Kitty to the more dignified Catherine. But more interesting is the treatment of the servants. In Jane Austen's published novels servants barely exist; they make occasional appearances where necessary to the action, but never feature in the cast of characters. The novels, it should be remembered, were published at the time when tunnels were being built in some country houses so that service and servants could move to and fro without being seen by the gentry. But one of the liveliest characters in *Catherine* is Mrs Percival's maid Anne – called Nanny by Catherine. When Edward Stanley makes his unexpected arrival, she comes rushing upstairs, and into Catherine's room, exclaiming,

'Lord Ma'am! Here's a gentleman in a chaise and four come, and I cannot for my life conceive who it is! I happened to be crossing the hall when the carriage drove up, and I knew nobody would be in the way to let him in but Tom, and he looks so awkward you know Ma'am, now his hair is just done up, that I was not willing the gentleman should see him, and so I went to the door myself. And he is one of the handsomest young men you would wish to see; I was almost ashamed of being seen in my apron, Ma'am, but however he is vastly handsome and did not seem to mind at all . . . However I thought he had better not come up into your dressing room, especially as everything is in such a litter, so I told him if he would be so obliging as to stay in the parlour, I would run up stairs and tell you he was come, and I dared to say that you would wait upon him. Lord Ma'am, I'd lay anything that he is come to ask you to dance with him tonight, and he's got his chaise ready to take you to Mr Dudley's.'

As Catherine comments 'Whoever he is, he has made a great impression on you, Nanny.'

The only servant in the published novels who talks at any length is, perhaps significantly, in the first of them, *Pride and Prejudice*, in the person of the house keeper at Pemberley; and she is not there in her own right but to serve a function, to give evidence of the good character of Mr Darcy. Her stately reflections do not bear comparison to the effervescence and vividness of Nanny's talk; with this it is as though a curtain has been drawn to give a momentary peep into life in Steventon Rectory as it was lived in the 1790s.

2

The myth of the Tennyson disinheritance

W HAT IS THAT gentle sound of rustling, clipping and scratching, that faint smell of burning, which the sensitive ear and nose can catch as background to the brassier sounds and smells of the decades around 1900? It is made by the widows and children of great Victorians at work deleting, cutting out and burning all the passages in letters, all the unpublished writings of parents or spouses which could deface the marble perfection of the portraits of greatness which they or suitably emasculated biographers are preparing for the world. Not always just the widows, for sometimes the act of purgation goes off while the great man himself, still magnificently bearded in his ruin, sits benignly in the background as the good work goes on.

The phalanx of industrious widows of great Victorians includes Edith Holman Hunt, whose ferocious blottings out in black ink were to frustrate and on occasions defeat the efforts of Diana Holman Hunt to reach to the true character of her grandfather; of Isabel Burton who certainly had plenty to hide about the dubious byways trodden by her husband Sir Richard Burton; and later Florence Hardy, whose efforts at canonisation first with the collaboration of her husband, and then after his death, were to inspire Somerset Maugham's best novel.

Queen Victoria, the most illustrious of the husband-sanctifying widows, presided over the five volumes of Theodore Martin's biography of the Prince Consort, and gave him a knighthood at the end of them; with the result, as Lytton Strachey put it, that 'an impeccable waxwork had been fixed by the Queen's love in the popular imagination, while the creature whom it represented – the real creature, so full of energy and stress and torment, so mysterious and so unhappy, and so fallible, and so very human – had altogether disappeared'. For the Queen herself a similar service was rendered by her daughter, Princess Beatrice, as with unflagging filial devotion she copied out all her mother's diaries, omitting anything which she thought unsuitable, and then destroyed the originals.

Prominent in the widows' club was the frail, ethereal, devoted, deeply conventional Emily Tennyson, aided by her dutiful younger son Lionel, who gave up his chances of an independent career to become, in effect, his father's unpaid secretary and biographer. In collaboration with his mother and with, it has to be admitted, the full support of his father, he destroyed two-thirds of Tennyson's available correspondence and edited what was allowed to survive. Other sources were carefully hand-picked, and the end result was *Alfred Lord Tennyson: a Memoir*, published in 1897, five years after the Poet Laureate had died. The modest title conceals two solid volumes, of over a thousand pages; it successfully discouraged any other biographer for fifty years. Their careful air-brushing had banished much of what made Tennyson interesting as a man and lay behind his poetry. Gone, as his later biographer Robert Bernard Martin puts it, was 'the rough Lincolnshire poet with his black blood, his inability to keep friendships cultivated, his reluctance to marry, his occasional obscenity and bad language, his terrible fits of depression, his obsessive fear of poverty, and his slowness to assume the responsibilities of maturity. Until his death there was constant scrubbing of his history going on in Farringford and Aldworth.'

Lionel Tennyson can be criticised for what he left out rather than for the inaccuracy of what he put in. The *Memoir*'s rambling miscellany of contents contains, in fact, much that is valuable and interesting. But at least one actual fallacy that he put in circulation deserves to be corrected, not least because it was attractively elaborated on by his nephew Sir Charles Tennyson, in his biography of 1949, and has been accepted as fact ever since.

Lionel briefly detailed how 'owing to a caprice of my great-grandfather's my grandfather, who was the elder son, was disinherited in favour of his only brother Charles', but compensated by being provided with several Church of England livings. Sir Charles expands on this. According to his biography, the poet's grandfather George Tennyson, who made the money, or most of it, 'made up his mind, while both his sons were still quite young, that the elder [the poet's father George] was not fitted to lead the Tennysons of the future by distinction and power, and that this destiny must be reserved for Charles. He also decided that the son who was not to be head of the family must go into the Church . . . George was a distinctly clever boy, yet he was sent first to a small school at York and then to a private tutor, whereas Charles was sent from York to Eton.' So George was sidetracked to vegetation in a country rectory at Somersby, whereas his brother Charles had a distinguished career in politics, inherited the bulk of his father's property, built a castellated country seat at Bayons Manor in Lincolnshire, and changed the family name to the grander one of Tennyson d'Eyncourt, to go with it. Charles flourished, while resentment at being disinherited was to obsess not only George, but all his many children, the poet included.

The story of George's disinheritance has been regularly repeated since Lionel first printed it and Sir Charles Tennyson further publicised it. When, in 1960, I visited Bayons Manor, then derelict, overgrown and far more amazing in ruin than it had ever been in its prime, and wrote about it in *Country Life*, I read Charles Tennyson's biography with delight, and my imagination was caught by the story as he told it. In my article I described how 'young George Tennyson was warped for life by this act of his father. His increasing bitterness and gloom, and ultimate drunkenness, the unhappiness and uneasiness of life at Somersby; the brood of Tennyson children, four daughters and seven huge and swarthy sons, packed uncomfortably into the vicarage, wandering across the Wolds in dirty clothes, singing poetry as they went, or sunk at times into a melancholy as deep as their father's, the ultimate glory of the rejected branch when Alfred Tennyson became one of the most famous Englishmen of the century – all this has become part of literary history.'

This is all very fine. But in fact George Tennyson was never disinherited. Charles Tennyson, and Lionel before him, took two undoubted facts, that old George Tennyson destined his elder son George for the Church in 1791, and that when he died in 1835 he left the bulk of his property to Charles, and without justification linked one to the other. Seen in the context of the time and his own position, what George the elder did in the 1790s was reasonable, and in no way unfavourable to his elder son.

George Tennyson descended from an undistinguished line of mainly professional men, and made his money as a solicitor in Market Rasen, a small town in Lincolnshire. It is true that his mother, heiress of the Clayton family of Grimsby merchants, had brought him considerable property in and around Grimsby; and that through her he also descended from the Hildyards, Lincolnshire gentry with grand medieval connections. But this, in terms of Lincolnshire county society, was little more than a gloss on the basic fact that he was what was called in the eighteenth century an attorney; and attorneys, as all readers of Jane Austen will know, were barely gentlemen (one of Mr Darcy's initial objections to Elizabeth Bennet was her low connections – an attorney's daughter as a mother and an attorney's wife as an aunt). Although George Tennyson was successfully acquiring property all over Lincolnshire, the increasing status which this could have given him was offset by disapproval of his unscrupulous business methods; to at least one of the Lincolnshire gentry he seemed a pushing obsequious rogue. When in the early years of their marriage he and his wife moved into one of the best houses in Lincoln, they were cold-shouldered by Lincoln society and retired discomfited to their home base at Grimsby.

In the late eighteenth century Church of England clergymen, unlike attorneys, were freely accepted as gentlemen – at least once they had acquired a living. Their social and economic position had been improving all through the century. Land enclosures had increased the size of tithes, which derived from land, and on which the clergy mainly depended for their income. The upper gentry and aristocracy, who often had the presentation of several livings, found that by combining two or more of them they could supply a comfortable berth for their younger sons. A lesser landowner with the presentation of one living only could conveniently increase his income by taking over the living himself, and becoming a 'Squarson' – a squire-cum-parson. The growing number of such socially acceptable parsons increased the standing of the whole order, with the result that prosperous self-made men began to send their sons into the Church to give them a step up socially. So, for example, George Austen, son of a surgeon, nephew of an attorney and of an apothecary, went into the Church, became rector of Steventon and Deane in Hampshire, married a woman of good family, moved, however modestly, in county society, and became the father of Jane, whose unfailing grasp of social nuances derived in part from her background.

In 1791 young George Tennyson was aged thirteen, his younger brother seven. It would have been unreasonably early in their lives for their father to disinherit the older one, and he did nothing of the sort. By buying him the reversion of two livings, he was doing what dozens of his contemporaries in a similar situation would have done. His elder son George would go into the Church and become a gentleman, free from any stigma of trade; his younger son, Charles, would join the family business. And this is what happened. George Junior was ultimately set up, on the basis of his vicarage at Somersby, with no fewer than five livings, bringing in an income of getting on for £1000 a year; Charles worked sedulously under his father in Market Rasen.

But over the decades there were important changes and developments in the Tennyson family. Old George grew steadily richer, acquired property all over Lincolnshire, and could leave enough behind him to set up both his sons in the landed gentry, if he so wanted. Charles married a rich wife, and George a poor one. In 1818 both George the elder and Charles were elected to Parliament. George did not stay in it for long, but for Charles it was the beginning of a political career; he cut loose from Market Rasen, was an MP for many years, representing four different constituencies, had a post in the Whig government as Clerk of the Ordnance from 1830 to 1832, and when he left office was made a Privy Counsellor. He moved between a house in South Street, Mayfair, and his father's house in Lincolnshire. His father was proud of him, though somewhat worried by the radical nature of his politics. On and off he quarrelled with him, for quarrelling and rows made up the atmosphere in which the Tennysons moved; but he got on much better with him than with

George. His relations with the latter were, on the whole, calamitous; both were difficult characters and George Junior was an epileptic and became an alcoholic; his own family as well as his father had a terrible time with him.

The elder George Tennyson was not an attractive character. He was an unscrupulous businessman and an impossible father and grandfather, by turns bullying, will-shaking, complaining, taking offence and indulging in self-pity. But, however difficult in language or letters, in his financial dealings he was scrupulously even-handed. There is no doubt that Charles was his favourite, but financially he was, if anything, more generous to George. He upped the allowance that he made him in stages to £1000 a year, more than he allowed to Charles; he paid (always complaining and lecturing) for additions to the rectory at Somersby, settled the considerable debts that Alfred and his elder brother Frederick ran up at Cambridge, paid the costs of their younger brother Edward when he had to go into an asylum (where he remained for the rest of his life), and one way and another was always bailing out the Somersby family. Individual members of it were invited in rotation over to his house at Tealby, to be vetted and exhorted by the 'Old Man of the Wolds', as the Somersby Tennysons called him.

In 1818 young George sent his eldest son, Frederick, to Eton. Sir Charles Tennyson is incorrect, in his biography, when he states, as an example of George's disinheritance, that Charles had been sent to Eton and George fobbed off with a local school; both brothers, in fact, went to St Peter's School in York. Frederick was the first Tennyson to go to Eton, and the only one of George's children to do so. The distinction seems an affirmation of his position as the eldest son of the eldest son; and, as he went with old George's approval, it must have seemed to the Somersby family that the old man recognised the situation, with all that it meant in terms of ultimate inheritance. Certainly (in spite of the accepted story) the younger George behaved like an elder son, and with a combined income of around £2000 a year could afford to do so. He added a mini-baronial hall to the rectory at Somersby; he filled it with a collection of dubious pictures bought in Italy; he kept a carriage. And Charles (in spite of the accepted story and his wife's money) behaved like an industrious younger son, with a career to make, first in his father's office, then, from the base of a modest house in Mayfair, in politics in London.

The Somersby Tennysons were popular in Lincolnshire country society – moving not in the grandest circles of the great landowners, but among the county gentry and clergy-men, the equivalent of the society in which the Austen family moved a generation earlier. Their father's admittedly appalling problems were mostly domestic; the face that he presented to the outside world was genial and amusing. The numerous Tennyson boys were considered odd but interest-ing; their swarthy good looks and the personable friends that they invited from Cambridge enlivened local dances.

Charles Tennyson and his father fitted much less well into the local gentry scene. Charles was disliked for two quite different reasons. His politics were radical; he supported Catholic Emancipation when the bulk of the upper classes were vitriolically opposed to it, stood up for George IV's estranged wife Caroline, whom they considered an impossi-ble German tart, and passed legislation to reform the game laws and prohibit spring traps, thus putting himself beyond the pale for all sporting landowners. At the same time he had what were considered absurd illusions about the importance of the Tennyson family through their shadowy connection with the medieval d'Eyncourts; in a jumped-up local lawyer these seemed both ridiculous and pretentious.

Old George Tennyson, on the other hand, after his one

abortive attempt to move in county circles in Lincoln, never showed much interest in socially integrating into the landed gentry, though his increasing wealth would have made this feasible enough if he had set his mind to it. His house at Tealby Lodge, later renamed Bayons Manor, was when he bought it little more than a thatched farmhouse, and he extended it in the same modest style, in spite of Charles's attempts to make him embark on something grander; the rectory at Somersby, with its Italian pictures and Gothic hall, had more pretensions. Old George seemed mostly concerned with amassing property and money for its own sake, and keeping his descendants guessing as to what he was going to do with them. He was sufficiently generous in making them allowances, which he could threaten to cut off, but grudged handing over more than the minimum of property or capital.

In 1831 the death of the younger George Tennyson, four years before that of his father, upset the lattter's carefully contrived financial equilibrium. Half the Somersby income vanished with his death; although he continued George's allowance to his widow (and even increased it), the Somersby family became a problem. The widow was a hopeless manager; her seven boys, instead of settling down to steady jobs, were improvident, wasteful, ran into debt, drank, suffered from melancholia and, almost worst of all, wrote poetry. Old George was in despair. Worst of all was Frederick, who, too conscious of being the eldest son of the eldest son, put on airs and had a relationship with his grandfather almost as bad as his father's had been – exacerbated, perhaps, by his nagging doubt that his grandfather was less interested in primogeniture than he was.

George worried about his son Charles too, but for different reasons. He saw that his political career was getting nowhere. He held the minor Government post of Clerk to the Ordnance for little more than a year, when he was dropped and fobbed off with the empty honour of being made a Privy Counsellor. His hopes of getting a peerage, or being made Speaker of the House of Commons, were probably held only by himself. In the summer of 1832 his father, now a widower and lonely, suggested that he abandoned London and came to live with him at Bayons. Frederick took this as an indication that he was going to make Charles his heir, and in July came over to Bayons and made a scene. Old George wrote to Charles how he had 'treated and left me in the most brutal manner. He is a savage . . . on his leaving me I said he would kill me by his conduct, his answering was "you will live long enough" . . . I have been at Rasen today and given instructions for an alteration to my will.'

Whatever may have been George's intentions (one could guess changing over the years), towards the end of 1833 he came out into the open; he moved out of Bayons to a smaller house that he owned nearby, and Charles and his wife moved in. When he died eighteen months or so later, Charles took over the arrangements at Bayons and, to misquote Alfred, 'the little church had seldom seen a costlier funeral'.

And now at last the final contents of the will, about which all the Tennysons had surmised for so long, were revealed. Frederick was by no means cut off with a shilling: the property which his grandfather had inherited at Grimsby, growing in value as new docks were built over it, was left to him, and supported him and his family in comfort over the years, first in a big villa in Florence, and then in the Channel Islands. Others of the Somersby Tennysons, including Alfred, got smaller legacies. But the rest of the estate, including Bayons and amounting to about three-quarters of the whole, went to Charles. He had, near enough, scooped the pool.

Old George had, according to his own lights, behaved with scrupulous correctness. His inherited property he left by primogeniture; the rest, which he had made himself, he left according to his own preferences. That was not how the Somersby Tennysons saw it. They bitterly resented what they considered their disinheritance, and continued to do so for many years. Echoes of their bitterness can be found in Tennyson's *Maud*, with its theme of wrongful wealth opposed to proud poverty, its tale of how

> . . . that old man, now lord of the broad estate and the hall
> Dropt off gorged from a scheme that had left us flaccid and drained.

What, in fact, does it matter whether the Somersby Tennysons were disinherited in 1791 or 1835 if, by and large, they were disinherited in the end? Yet it is always worth righting stories that have been mistold; not least because in this case the wrong telling has done an injustice to the 'Old Man of the Wolds'. Unattractive though he may have been, he was not as bad as he has been painted.

3

Up and down with Oscar Wilde

THE STORY of Oscar Wilde's rise, catastrophe and decline is one of the best-known dramas of the late nineteenth century. But there must always be a tendency, to which Wilde himself gave way, to accentuate the drama by exaggerating both his rise and his fall. For if one looks into it, the success was not as great, and the decay not as miserable, as he and others have portrayed it. This essay is not concerned with any evaluation of what he wrote or said; it merely tries to chart the technique of self-promotion used by an Irishman on the climb in London, and to look at the finances of his decline in Paris.

Since it deals with his less attractive aspects, perhaps it is worth, as a preliminary antidote, quoting from one of his letters as a reminder of the zest and bubbling sense of fun that could make him so irresistible (of people I have known, only John Betjeman had something of the same quality). The letter is to young Campbell Dodgson, who had spent a few days in 1893 tutoring Alfred Douglas for his Oxford exams, in the house that Wilde had rented at Babbacombe, on the edge of Torquay.

> I am still conducting the establishment on the old lines and really think I have succeeded in combining the advantages of a public school with those of a private lunatic asylum, which, as you know, was my aim . . .

All the boys of the school send their best love, and kindest wishes.

Sincerely yours,
Oscar Wilde
Headmaster, Babbacombe School

Babbacombe School
Headmaster – Mr Oscar Wilde
Second Master – Mr Campbell Dodgson
Boys – Lord Alfred Douglas

Rules
Tea for masters and boys at 9.30 a.m.
Breakfast at 10.30
Work 11.30–12.30
At 12.30 Sherry and biscuits for headmaster and boys (the second master objects to this)
12.40–1.30. Work
1.30. Lunch
2.40–4.30.Compulsory hide-and-seek for headmaster
5. Tea for headmaster and second master, brandy and sodas (not to exceed seven) for boys.
6–7. Work
7.30 Dinner, with compulsory champagne.
8.30–12. Ecarte, limited to five-guineas points
12–1.30. Compulsory reading in bed. Any boy found disobeying this rule will be immediately woken up.
At the conclusion of the term the headmaster will be presented with a silver inkstand, the second master with a pencil-case, as a token of esteem, by the boys.

When Wilde embarked on his English career as an undergraduate at Magdalen in 1874, he was starting from scratch.

In Ireland his parents were well-known characters, his father an eminent surgeon, antiquarian and womaniser, his mother a poet and Dublin hostess. Wilde himself had been a star as a student at Trinity College Dublin. All this counted for nothing in England, where no one had heard of his parents or of him. He had to make his own way, and be his own promoter and advertiser. This was something that came easily to him.

His cleverness (a double first), vitality and ambition made its mark at Oxford; he became sufficiently well known for the University Chaplain to deliver a sermon rebuking the young man (unnamed) who said that he had to live up to his blue china – 'there has crept into these cloistered shades a form of heathenism'. But from early on he set out to establish a wider reputation by means of his poems and articles. He sedulously sent copies of these, published or unpublished, to eminent people, with an accompanying letter, on the lines of 'I am only a shy young poet/student, but wish to pay tribute to your genius.' Gladstone got two of these; other recipients in his early years included Matthew Arnold, W. H. Rossetti, Lord Houghton, G. F. Watts and Swinburne.

His Magdalen friends were not to play much of a part in his post-Oxford life. Much more important was Frank Miles, a young man two years older than Wilde; he was not at the university, though Wilde may first have met him at Oxford, probably in the summer of 1876. The Mileses were by origin Bristol bankers who had made money and branched out into the surrounding counties, buying estates and buying or building country houses. They had the wealth and connections that Wilde lacked. Miles's father was an Anglican clergyman, who had built one of the best Victorian churches in Bristol at his own expense. His wife, daughter and son were all artistically inclined. Their rectory at Bingham in Nottinghamshire became for a time a surrogate home for Wilde, but Frank was his especial friend. He had studied at the Royal Academy Schools, and by the time that Wilde met him was establishing a reputation with pretty if pallid portraits of professional beauties, which were sold in large numbers in reproduction and published in the illustrated magazines. He had been taken up by Lord Ronald Gower, brother of the Duke of Sutherland, amateur sculptor, and (as Miles's parents were unlikely to have realised) doyen of the crypto-homosexual world in London.

When Wilde left Oxford he moved with him into rooms in Salisbury Street off the Strand, while Miles waited for the completion of the studio house that he was building in Tite Street, Chelsea. It was designed by E. W. Godwin, Whistler's friend and one of the most advanced architects of the day, and was opposite Whistler's own White House, also designed by Godwin. Miles and Wilde moved into the new house in August 1880.

Miles was important in Wilde's career for three reasons. Through him he had access to the heart of the Aesthetic Movement, in which both Whistler and Godwin were central figures. Miles may have given him an entrée to homosexual circles in London, and certainly introduced him to his set of fashionable or notorious ladies; they came to parties in Salisbury Street or Tite Street, and Lily Langtry, in particular, fell for Wilde, and may even have had an affair with him. She probably brought her lover, the Prince of Wales, to Tite or Salisbury Streets on at least one occasion, enabling Wilde, with the Atlantic safely between them, to refer to 'my friend the Prince of Wales' when lecturing to Californian miners in 1882.

His friendship with Lily Langtry brought Wilde cachet: homosexual London was ultimately to destroy him, but initially it was Miles's Aesthetic connections which were of the most importance to him. It must have been due to Miles and Ronald Gower that in 1877, while still at Oxford, he reviewed the opening exhibition at the Grosvenor Gallery, the Aesthetic Movement's answer to the Royal Academy.

When he moved in with Miles in London he threw himself all out into the Aesthetic Movement, and set out to publicise himself as its propagator. He sedulously attended public events and private parties, long-haired, aesthetically attired and attended by a circle of adoring young women also in aesthetic outfits, to whom he expounded his views. His behaviour amused some and infuriated others, but it succeeded in establishing his image with the media and the London public as a representative young aesthete. When his poems were published in 1881, *Punch* had a cartoon of a sunflower, the flower favoured by aesthetes, with Wilde's face as its centre. It continued to satirise him in articles and cartoons. In Frith's painting of *A Private View at the Royal Academy, 1881*, the most prominent feature was, as Frith put it, 'a well-known apostle of the beautiful, with a herd of eager worshippers surrounding him'. This was of course Wilde. He got himself widely accepted as the original of the poet Bunthorne in Gilbert's *Patience*, although this was not the case. His final triumph was to be sent out by the D'Oyly Carte company on a lecture tour in America, to coincide with a tour of the company. So, in full aesthetic rig of long hair, knee breeches, floppy tie and ribboned shoes, he set out to conquer America. He had by now fallen out with Frank Miles, whose father had taken exception to some of the 1881 poems, and forced his son to stop sharing the house in Tite Street with him. But, in terms of Wilde's career, Miles had served his purpose.

In one way the American tour, successful though it was, was a mistake. Wilde was away in America for a year, and in Paris for three months. He came back to find that his public had moved on. The Aesthetic Movement was no longer news. An English lecture tour proved much less successful than the

American one. He had long since got rid of his small Irish inheritance, and quickly spent the money that he had brought back from America. In 1884 he married Constance Lloyd, shy, pretty, determined and with £900 a year. The marriage started with a good deal of idealism on both sides, but the £900 played a part. It did not go far, however, to finance Wilde's expansive tastes. It could not build him a new house, and he had to content himself with an undistinguished one in a terrace down the road from his old berth in Tite Street; although he had it decorated by Godwin it excited only a modest amount of attention. His marriage was not going well. Debts mounted up, and he had to take a job as editor of a women's magazine, which brought him little prestige and which soon bored him.

Wilde's poetry was not very good. In the Aesthetic Movement he was a populariser not an originator; his ideas and even his clothes had been pioneered by others. *The Happy Prince*, his book of children's stories which he published in 1888, was certainly charming, and in January 1889 his magazine essay 'The Decay of Lying' caused something of a stir. As a talker he continued to dazzle, delight, and sometimes irritate. But it might have seemed that, now conventionally dressed and with his hair cut (although still waved), he was settling down as an amusing show-off and minor literary figure. Then he published *The Portrait of Dorian Gray*.

Dorian Gray was first published in *Lippincott's Magazine*, in England and America, in June 1890, and then in book form, enlarged, in May 1891. Wilde wrote, shortly before its Lippincott publication, 'I think it will make a sensation.' It was designed to attract attention, and succeeded. The reviews were all that author and publishers could have hoped for: 'A poisonous book'; 'Why go grubbing in muck heaps?'; 'a work of art'; 'wonderful spirited insight'; 'the commonplace is scarcely possible to him'; 'unmanly, sickening, vicious and tedious', and so on. It may have been more written about than read (it was 1895 before it went into a second edition; Stevenson's *Jekyll and Hyde*, which in part inspired it, sold far more copies), but it was undoubtedly a book of the year. At the end of May 1891, Wilde was invited to Taplow Court by Mrs William Grenfell, one of the leaders of Society.

It is hard to realise today how formidable and impressive Society with a capital S seemed to those who were not in it. It was to come through the 1914–18 war, but cracked and reduced; it survived the 1939–45 war in tatters, if at all. But in the 1880s and 1890s it seemed unassailable. It owned most of the land in England, Scotland, Wales and Ireland, and all the best houses both in London and the countryside, crammed with amazing possessions and obsequious servants. In politics the Cabinet was largely its preserve, and it had a monopoly of Prime Ministers, Viceroys and Governor Generals. Its members, as sleek, gleaming and well groomed as their horses and carriages, moved with self-confidence through the allotted social round: the Season in London, the Eton and Harrow Match, Ascot, Goodwood and Cowes, perhaps an outing to Marienbad, Italy or Egypt, then hunting and shooting from their own country houses or those of their relatives or friends.

To gain entry into Society, if one was not born into it, was possible and simple. All that was necessary was to buy an estate of five thousand acres or so, buy or build a country house to go with it, send one's sons to Eton or Harrow, have one's daughters presented at Court, and one was in – or at least one's children were. But to those who could not up the ante, it seemed unassailable.

Society was more approachable in London than in the country. Those of its members who had a taste for that kind of thing invited outsiders – lawyers, writers, artists, even actors – to their dinners or receptions, though not to their dances. With rare exceptions, they did not invite them to their country houses. Only a few were given the entrée to those, for reasons not always clear – Landseer but not Millais, Dickens but not Thackeray, Lear but not Carroll, Tennyson but not Browning, Barrie and James but not Galsworthy or Hardy. Those invited were usually safely married or considered unlikely to want to marry, for one of the functions of Society's social round and house parties was to marry off one's children to other members of Society, preferably elder sons or heiresses. Every mother's bad dream was a misalliance.

Of the country houses the guests at whose 'Saturday to Monday' parties ('weekend' was considered a vulgar expression) were recorded in the *Morning Post*, none was better known or more select than Taplow Court, and no one more admired than its chatelaine, Ettie Grenfell – soon to be Lady Desborough. Its glamour is immortalised in one of Max Beerbohm's best stories, 'Maltby and Braxton', in which Taplow Court features as Keeb Hall and Mrs Grenfell as the Duchess of Hertfordshire.

The story deals with Hilary Maltby who has written a bestseller, *Ariel in Mayfair*. At the Annual Soirée of the Inkwomen's Club he meets the duchess, who, on the strength of one little poem in *The Gentlewoman*, had been unanimously elected an Honorary Vice-President of the Club. She gushes and invites him to Keeb. By a mean trick he dissuades her from also inviting Stephen Braxton, the author of the rival bestseller *A Faun in the Cotswolds*.

'Arcady, Olympus, the right people at last.' He buys three new summer suits, a new evening suit, some new white waistcoats and a smoking suit. Also a new dressing case, to impress the footman who unpacks for him ('It looked compromisingly new . . . I had to kick it industriously, and throw it about and scratch it, so as to avert possible suspicion'). He packs a supply of letters, to answer on Keeb writing paper, and, as requested, takes his bicycle – bicycling is Society's new craze. And so the 3.30 from Victoria finds him, his bicycle in the van, in a carriage of 'tall, cool, ornate people' bound for Keeb. Monday's newspapers list the guests: the Austro-Hungarian Ambassador, the Duke and Duchess of Mull, four lesser Peers (two of them Proconsuls, however) with their Peeresses, three Peers without their Peeresses, four Peeresses without their Peers, a dozen bearers of courtesy titles, and finally Mr A. J. Balfour, Mr Henry Chaplin and Mr Hilary Maltby.

The visit is a disaster, because at key moments the wraith of Braxton unexpectedly startles him into a series of faux-pas. Things seem to pick up when the bossy Lady Rodfitton takes an interest in him, discusses his projected new book, and suggests that they go bicycling together. As they tool along the terrace, Maltby finds himself rehearsing a dedication:

TO ELEANOR
COUNTESS OF RODFITTON
THIS BOOK WHICH OWES ALL
TO HER WISE COUNSEL
AND UNWEARYING SUPERVISION
IS GRATEFULLY DEDICATED
BY HER FRIEND
THE AUTHOR

Alas, the wraith of Braxton jumps out of the bushes, causing Maltby to swerve, crash into the Countess's bicycle, and over-turn her.

Beerbohm was writing in about 1915, relaxed after fifteen years or so of regular visits to Taplow, and remembering with amusement his first excursions into the country-house world. Here, for instance, is a letter written by him to Reginald Turner in 1898, not from Taplow but from Sir William Eden's Windelstone Hall:

Observe the notepaper. I write from the Stately Home of a Baronet of Jacobite creation, Sir William Eden in the County of Durham . . . I have a smoking suit of purple with dark red facings . . . the house is very comfortable and distinguished. In the Hall is a Visitors' Book over which I spend most of my leisure moments – a Debrett in ms. The dear Ormonds, the dear Londonderrys, the dear Zetlands and many others too numerous and too distinguished for me to mention.

All this is reminiscent of Wilde at Taplow and elsewhere. Before his anni mirabiles of 1890–91, his visits to the great had been confined to stays with the Duke of Newcastle at Clumber in 1886 and 1888, and a visit to his brother at Deepdene, in 1889. The two names were dropped casually into his correspondence: 'I am keeping the book for study in the Clumber woods next week'; 'I was away at Clumber and unable to come and see you'; 'I have only just returned from Deepdene'. But they were not as impressive as they sounded. He owed them less to his own reputation than to his friend Carlos Blacker, who was also a friend of the Duke's. The latter was a sad young man, deeply religious and a cripple from childhood, who was living at Clumber at half-cock, trying to pay off the debts left by his father. His brother, on the other hand, was a rake, rapidly heading for bankrupty. For Wilde neither relationship survived their marriages.

But in 1890 the success of the Lippincott *Dorian Gray* had already led to visits to two baronets in Scotland, with excursions to surrounding country houses. Taplow followed in May 1891, and in August he was invited to Wrest Park in Bedfordshire by Lady Cowper, Mrs Grenfell's aunt and equally renowned as a hostess. In July Wilfrid Scawen Blunt invited him to the Crabbet Club, the weekend gathering of his young aristocratic admirers, held at Crabbet Park in Sussex, to celebrate his birthday. In November he was entertained by the Earl and Countess of Lytton at the British Embassy in Paris. In London the great were suddenly eager to meet him.

The all too inevitable result followed when his second book of children's stories, *The House of Pomegranates*, was published in November. The book as a whole was dedicated to his wife, but the four stories each had individual dedications. These were not to friends of many years, such as Helena Sickert, Ellen Terry, Frances Forbes-Robertson or Katie Lewis, who loved him and to whom he wrote some of his most delightful letters, but to 'Margaret Lady Brooke' (the Ranee of Sarawak), 'Mrs William H. Grenfell of Taplow Court', 'H.S.H. Alice, Princess of Monaco', and 'Miss Margot Tennant', Society's new exploding firework, who was shortly to have a best-selling novel written in her celebration.

To the best of my knowledge no account of Wilde at Taplow has come to light; but his visit to Wrest is described in an unfriendly letter from 'Doll' Riddell, who was one of the house party:

> Mr Wilde came. He was a great talker and raconteur, and occasionally said good things. The only one which I remember is that he said there ought to be 'a Form of Prayer used for a Baronet'. In the afternoon he sat on the lawn, surrounded by a large audience of ladies, to whom he told stories. His signing of the visitors' book was characteristic. It was a huge tome, with large, thick, creamy sheets. He did not sign on the same sheet as the rest of the party, but took a fresh sheet, on which he wrote his name towards the top, and then executed an immense flourish, so that no other name could be written on the same page.

The Crabbet outing was in some ways a disaster. Any

newcomer to the Club had to be introduced. Wilde's sponsor was George Nathaniel Curzon, with whom he had had friendly relations at Oxford, which had seemed to continue. Bu there was a streak of treachery in Curzon. His introduction, under a veneer of jocularity, tore Wilde to shreds, and not just with insinuations about his homosexuality. Wilde, in Blunt's words, 'sat helplessly smiling, a fat mass, in his chair'. He made a good recovery, got up to speak in his turn, and had his own fun with Curzon. But he did not come back to Crabbet.

The Lytton meeting took place because Lord Lytton had been understandably delighted with Wilde's 'The Decay of Lying' when it was published with other essays in book form as *Intentions* in May 1891. He wrote to Wilde suggesting that he let him know if he was ever planning a visit to Paris. Wilde answered in terms that suggest that he hoped for an invitation to stay. In fact nothing materialised until 2 November, when Wilde went to the Embassy, but only to lunch. The lunch was described by Lytton's daughter Emily (later to be married to Edwin Lutyens). 'We all thought him very amusing and not so odious as we expected, though he is evidently fearfully conceited. He talked chiefly about his own health and his books, but he was certainly amusing.'

At the time of the lunch, Lytton was already sick of a mysterious malady. Wilde may have paid further visits to him, but he died three weeks later. It must have been delightful for Wilde to be taken up by an Earl, Ambassador, ex-Viceroy of India, with Disraeli and D'Orsay lurking in his background, and his death was a grievous shock. He wrote accordingly to Lady Dorothy Nevill, somewhat exaggerating the six-month relationship. 'I would have answered your charming letter before, but the death of poor dear Lytton has quite upset me. We had become during the last year very great friends, and I had seen him only a few days before he died, lying in Pauline Borghese's lovely room at the Embassy, and full of charm and grace and tenderness'.

Visits to Lytton ceased of necessity; visits to Taplow and Wrest need not have ceased, but in fact did so. He was not asked to them again, or to any other great house. Hesketh Pearson, the most sympathetic and readable, but not the most accurate, of his biographers, states: 'It must be remembered that he was thoroughly spoilt by the aristocracy . . . and was a welcome visitor at the town and country houses of half the nobility,' but it was not the case. He had failed to make it with the upper classes.

Did this matter? Perhaps 90 per cent of what was worth-while or entertaining in science, literature and the arts took place outside Society; perhaps 90 per cent of its members were not very interesting. It did matter, however, because it was important to Wilde. He would dearly have loved to be on the inside. Part of the glamour, for him, of his relationship with Lord Alfred Douglas was that Douglas was a lord. The dedications continued, in the two of his plays that were pub-lished in his lifetime: *Lady Windermere's Fan* to 'the Dear Memory of Robert Earl of Lytton in Affection and Admira-tion'; *A Woman of No Importance* to 'Gladys, Countess de Grey'. The plays were firmly set in Society. There are two titled characters in *Dorian Gray*; there are nine in *Lady Windermere's Fan*. Wilde's own self-portraits in the plays were ennobled as Lord Henry Wotton, Lord Illingworth and Lord Goring.

Society continued to meet Wilde at dinners in London, and flocked to the plays, to enjoy and to laugh at them. But when disaster struck in 1895 it was Wilde's middle-class friends who stood by him. The nobs, with the honourable exception of the Ranee of Sarawak, could not wait to drop him.

II

A scene, with variations, occurs in a number of memoirs of the period. The writers are walking in Paris when an unkempt figure lurches out of the shadows and asks them for money. Horrified, they realise that it is Oscar Wilde. They press a coin into his hand, and he staggers into the dark again.

Distressing scenes of this nature undoubtedly occurred but, as his biographers make clear, Wilde was by no means permanently down and out in Paris. But no one, to my knowledge, has added up, in print at least, the total amount of his income in the three and a half years between his coming out of prison on 19 May 1897, and his death in Paris on 30 November 1900.

Wilde's basic income in this period was the £150 a year, paid quarterly, allowed to him by his wife, and by trustees after his wife's death. The allowance was withheld for some months in 1897–98, owing to his going to live with Alfred Douglas in Naples, but the backlog was paid after they separated. The income (which needs to be multiplied by perhaps 70 to get its modern equivalent) should have been enough to support a single man living modestly in Paris, but there was never any chance of 'my wretched three pounds a week', as Wilde referred to it, being enough for someone of his tastes and nature. It did not, in fact, have to be so.

When he came out of prison he was presented with £800, which had been collected for him by his friends. In December 1897 and January 1898 Lady Queensberry paid him £200 on condition of his leaving her son, and she and Alfred Douglas gave him a further £1000 in the course of 1900 (the death of Lord Queensberry in January had released capital to them). Wilde, not unreasonably, took much of this last payment as money due to him, since in 1895 Douglas's elder brother had promised to pay Wilde's legal costs, and had not done so. In addition, Frank Harris provided at least £50 to support him when he stayed in the south of France at the beginning of 1899, and Harold Mellor contributed £50 towards his visit to Italy in the summer of 1900. Finally, small gifts, sometimes disguised as loans, from Robbie Ross, Reggie Turner, Frank Harris, George Ives, John Rothenstein and Alfred Douglas, brought in at least £120 over the years. After *The Ballad of Reading Gaol* Wilde wrote nothing, but his literary earnings, from the *Ballad*, reprints of other works, and advances for works unwritten were not inconsiderable. The *Ballad* itself was, in his lifetime, his only big seller, running into seven editions, mostly of a thousand copies; but its selling price was very small, and if, as Wilde wrote, he only got threepence for each copy sold, his royalties are unlikely to have been much more than £80. In September 1897 Dalhousie Young paid him a £100 advance for a projected libretto which was never written. In April 1899 he sold his rights in the book versions of *The Ideal Husband* and *The Importance of Being Ernest* to Leonard Smithers for £30. In 1900 George Alexander, who had bought the acting rights of two of Wilde's plays at the time of his bankruptcy in 1895, started to put the plays on again and volunteered to make Wilde ex-gratia payments from his profits. He paid him £100 in that year, and had Wilde lived these payments would have been a useful supplement to his income.

But Wilde's biggest literary earnings came from his projected writing of the play that came to be called *Mr and Mrs Daventry*. This was first sketched out as early as 1894; the project was taken up again when he came out of prison, but in the end Wilde only contributed the plot, and the play was written by Frank Harris and produced, with some success, in October 1900. In the interval, however, Wilde had raised £500 or so by accepting advances of £100 from at least four different people, without telling Harris or the others what he was doing.

These various sums add up as follows: £525 from his allowance, £810 in literary earnings, and over £2200 in gifts etc. from other sources, a total of £3535, or around £1000 a year – around £70,000 a year in modern values.

Of course, apart from his allowance, the rest came in at irregular intervals, and Wilde being Wilde, whatever came in he spent immediately, mostly on booze or boys. It was in the intervals, when he was distressed for money and had no qualms in cadging from whoever was available, that the distressing scenes took place. And face to face or in letters he continuously lamented his lack of funds. 'Like dear St Francis of Assisi,' he wrote, 'I am wedded to Poverty; but in my case the marriage is not a success.' He escaped from it, though, rather more often than he let on.

4

Yonghy-Bonghy-Wilde

I WAS INTRIGUED to notice that Edward Lear gives his Yonghy-Bonghy-Bo the features and long hair of Oscar Wilde. The two men came from different generations and different backgrounds, and any connection between them might seem unlikely. In 1877, the year in which the Yonghy poem was published, Wilde was still at Oxford and barely known in London.

A possible link exists, however, in the form of Violet, Slingsby, Guy and Lionel, whose adventures had been celebrated in one of Lear's nonsense stories, published in 1871 as 'The Story of the Four Little Children who went round the World'. This was written for the four children of a London lawyer, Slingsby Bethell: Violet, born in 1859, the twins Slingsby and Guy, born in 1861, and Lionel, born in 1864. By 1880 Wilde and the Bethells were living a few doors away from each other in Tite Street, Chelsea, Wilde sharing the house which his friend Frank Miles had built in 1878–79, the Bethells in a house bought in 1879 from Archibald Stuart-Wortley and Carlo Pellegrini, better known as the cartoonist Spy.

In the late 1870s Tite Street was being developed or colonised by those in sympathy with the Aesthetic Movement. Their god was Whistler, whose White House stood opposite Frank Miles's; Slingsby Bethell had already had designs made for a site immediately next door to it, but these fell through and he acquired the Stuart-Wortley/Pellegrini house instead. All the Tite Street people already knew each other, or were likely to have done so, before they moved in there.

Wilde's Aesthetic period dates from in or around 1876, when he first got to know Frank Miles; and in his later Oxford years he was adventuring into London society, and beginning to make an impact on young girls in it, some of whom became his devoted admirers and others found him 'awful'. Mrs Jingly Jones, the Yonghy-Bonghy-Bo's inamorata, is portrayed by Lear in full Aesthetic-Kate-Green-away rig. Could she have been modelled on Violet Bethell, who did not marry until 1888, and in the 1870s presumably lived with her parents? Could Lear have come across Wilde in the Bethells' house?

5

Walter wins: a hunt but no kill

WALTER CLAIMED to have had sex with at least 1200 women, including 'Negresses, Mulattos, Creoles, Indian half-breeds, Greeks, Armenians, Turks, Egyptians, Hindus and squaws of the wild American and Canadian races', and women from every nation in Europe except Lapland. His only racial prejudice seems to have been against Irish women, 'having generally found them the lowest, bawdiest, foulest-tongued, blarneying, lying, cheating, as well as the dirtiest of all the harlots'.

But he did not confine himself to harlots. Whenever anyone, of any class, in any place, at any time, appealed to him he went flat out at them: at farm workers whom he met on country roads or in the fields, at shop assistants in London or elsewhere, at circus performers, at the maidservants in his own family houses, or the houses of relatives or friends, at the wives or daughters of these friends and relatives, at fellow guests in hotels, at the wife of a Northern manufacturer in London (he had a son by her) and at an Italian marchesa in Rome. He frequented prostitutes all round the world, and with some of them formed long-lasting relationships. He must have been attractive and full of vitality; it is remarkable (if what he wrote is to be relied upon) how often apparent rectitude and respectability melted before his advances.

'Walter' is a pseudonym, adopted for the original publication of *My Secret Life* in eleven volumes containing 4200 pages, apparently in Amsterdam c. 1882–94. It purports to have an editor, to whom 'Walter' had entrusted the manuscript, but this may be a subterfuge. Only six sets are said to have been printed. It was not reprinted until 1966, when the Grove Press of New York issued the whole text in two handsome volumes. England was less tolerant. When the Press's English agent, Arthur Dobson, issued the first two volumes of the original on his own account in 1969, he was prosecuted and given a two-year sentence as 'a professional purveyor of filth'.

Dobson may have been encouraged by the previous English publication of 'Walter' by Polybooks of London in or soon after 1967. Polybooks got away with it because *My Secret Life* was not published neat, but in extracts diluted by a copious introduction and annotations supplied by Drs Eberhard and Phyllis Kronhauser, 'prominent psychologists and sexologists' in America. This gave it just enough respectability as a work of academic research to avoid prosecution. The two volumes, and a third that followed in 1970, were much in circulation at the time. They were my first introduction to Walter. One could skip the Dr Kronhausers' lengthy expositions and go straight to the dirty bits.

Walter would have denied the word 'dirty', or any accusation that he was a pornographer. He stuck up for himself. He was doing no more than 'obeying the divine law that draws men and women together in carnal union'. 'Women have been the greatest joy of my life and are so to every true man from infancy to old age. Copulation is the highest pleasure both to the body and mind, and is worth all the other pleasures put together.' 'Moreover,' he wrote, 'it seems to me that both men and women may be straight and fair in all they do, be as good and useful members of society as others, yet take their chief delight in carnal pleasures.' He stuck up for prostitutes too. 'They have been my refuge in sorrow, an unfailing relief in all my miseries, have saved me from drinking, gambling and perhaps worse. I shall never throw stones at them, nor speak hastily to them or of them.'

But Walter was a man of his time. He was – or at least became – a compulsive collector and cataloguer as well as a womaniser. Like the Victorian geologists who went all over the world tapping at rocks or collecting fossils, or the naturalists who sailed like Darwin in search of animal and plant specimens to analyse and catalogue, Walter went round the world collecting women, not only fucking them but watching them being fucked by others, interested in every variety of sexual behaviour, ready to have a go at it himself and writing it all down in his diary. He was a dedicated worker and happy in his work.

He would surely have been pleased to have been described, as he has been, as 'a pioneer apostle of sexual freedom', 'a pioneer sexologist' writer of 'the most important document of its type about Victorian England', 'a true forerunner of both Freud and Kinsey', 'a fearless fighter against prudery, hypocrisy and fake shame' and to know that he features in *The Oxford Dictionary of National Biography*, one of only two anonymous characters to be included in it, with a full and respectful entry by Professor Brian Harrison, eminent social historian and the editor of the *Dictionary*.

One can be a little sceptical of efforts to elevate Walter's compulsive urges, and to present him as a pioneer and public benefactor. In spite of a surface kindliness he never allowed any consideration for others to divert him from pursuing his own self-gratification. But his autobiography is more than endless descriptions of the sexual act, which, as he honestly admits, can grow monotonous. His women are not just bodies but individuals: he can bring to life people and places in a few words of vivid description, so that the reader feels that he is there himself, watching or listening in.

But who was Walter? G. Legman, in the preface to the two-volume New York edition, suggested that he was Henry Spencer Ashbee, father of C. R. Ashbee, the Arts and Crafts designer, but well known in his own right – as Fiona McCarthy puts it in her biography of his son – as 'one of the most avid collectors of erotic literature the world has ever seen' (he left his collection to the British Museum). This desire to identify Walter with a celebrity is on a par with attempts to identify Jack the Ripper with Walter Sickert or the Duke or Clarence. There is not a jot of supporting evidence in the *Secret Life* itself; it gives the impression of being written by a much less educated Victorian businessman than Ashbee, and one only marginally interested in erotic literature.

Gordon Grimley in his good introduction to the Panther Books selection, published in 1972, tentatively suggests another Victorian businessman and collector of erotica, William S. Potter, but produces no very good reasons to convince even himself: he opens his introduction by stating that 'no one knows, and no one is now ever likely to discover, the identity of the author of *My Secret Life*'. Brian Harrison, in his *ODNB* entry, by and large says the same. But Legman, Grimley and Harrison all accept that it is a real diary or auto-biography, not fantasy – basically on the grounds that that is how it reads. And when one reads it one finds oneself agree-ing with them.

I keep the three volumes of the Kronhausen Walter along with my other paperback biographies, on a bookshelf in the bathroom, immediately next to the lavatory. As they begin with W they are very much to hand on the bottom shelf, alongside the Rev. F. E. Witts's *Diary of a Cotswold Parson* and Bernard Walke's *Twenty Years at St Hilary*. Over the years I occasionally dip into them, even though the volumes are irritating to read because they have fallen to pieces – not through excessive use, but because they were badly bound.

The *Diary* is full of dashes, to help the atmosphere of anonymity. In browsing one day I happened to notice that the Lord E - - t - r, with whom Walter was acquainted, and who kept Eliza F - - - m - - g in a villa in Regents Park, could only be the 2nd Marquess of Exeter – from what I knew of him, this was no surprise. A little later came a passing reference to Mrs O - b - - n -, with whom Walter had had an affair in a hotel in Switzerland. Could this possibly be Mrs Osborne, of Newtown Anner in Ireland, where my grandmother and aunt used to live? I knew she was a stormy character, who used to holiday in Switzerland and had the worst possible relationship with her husband, the politician Ralph Bernal Osborne.

I had not previously paid much attention to the dashed names, which I had presumed were fabrications, but on looking a little closer it was obvious that many of them, at least, were not. Some of them, place names and names of streets especially, were transparently identifiable, and there seemed in fact little point in Walter having used them. When describing himself as going to the English seaside, or up to Scotland, or travelling in Italy or Spain, why bother, except in order to create a general air of mystification, to change Margate into M - - g - - e, or Edinburgh into E - - - b - - - h or Florence and Rome into F - - r - - - e and R - - e, or Gibraltar into G - - r - - t - r?

But it occurred to me that if I went to the complete edition and combed through *all* the blanks, instead of a small selection, I might find sufficient pointers to enable me to identify Walter. I realised that this, and research into Walter generally, could be full of pitfalls, of jumps when one could never knew if one's taking off place was firm. According to Walter's editor, or Walter himself if the editor is a fabrication, although the incident related in the *Diary* and the people involved are all genuinely depicted, locations are sometimes changed, and details altered: 'The district is sometimes given wrongly; but it matters little whether Brompton be substituted for Hackney, or Camden Town for Walworth . . . I have mystified family affairs, but if I say I had ten cousins when I had but six, or that one aunt's house was in Surrey, instead of Kent, or in Lancashire, it breaks the clue and cannot matter to the reader.' And 'initials are always the true ones'.

Anyway, I spent a bit of time going through the complete New York edition at the supervised desk in the British Library. This, according to accounts, used to be a somewhat off-putting experience, involving working under the beady and suspicious eye of a supervisor on the lookout to see if one was cutting out pages or scribbling obscenities on them. Nowadays it is relaxed enough: the table is shared with readers of musical scores and no one appears to take much interest in what one is doing.

But I did not get much out of it. The 'well-known courtesan S - - t - - s who took a fancy to me but her foul tongue shocked me' was, of course, Skittles, whose tongue was later to delight Wilfred Scawen Blunt. Another courtesan, picked up in the Argyle Rooms, was N - - l - e H - - - - s who gave him the clap, and whom he met four years later 'superb in jewels' at a public ball, and who then married Lord R - - - - s: she was Nellie Homes, alias Eleanor Suter, who married Lord Rivers in 1845. The Duke of R - - - - - - d, another frequenter of ladies of this type, could only be the Duke of Richmond. Mrs O - b - - n - , perhaps Osborne, turned out to be from New Orleans, not from Ireland. All this was mildly interesting, but did not help towards identifying Walter himself. What it did do, I suppose, was to warm me up for a Walter hunt.

The next stage was more exciting. Walter goes into some detail about his early years. His parents lived in affluence and comfort – one got the impression of unearned income (for his father was always at home) – in a house with stables and grooms adjoining. Then his father got into financial difficulties, went off for a year to look after 'some plantations', came back a sick and broken man, and soon died, on the verge of bankruptcy. Before he died the family had moved into a smaller house in the suburbs of London, and after his death his mother was left in reduced circumstances. Walter attended a neighbouring 'great school or college' as a day boy.

The situation of this house is described in some detail in an episode in the *Secret Life*. Walter, having come into money and wasted it, went back to stay with his mother, who was still living in the same house. It was the last of a row and along one side of it ran a lane which went through a field and gardens for some way, then crossed a road, went in to the very large churchyard, only half-filled, of a church, and joined the high road. The lane was little used, except on Sundays and 'by lovers who walked there on summer nights'.

Walter, on this visit, followed two laundrywomen and their cart up the lane, through the churchyard and into the high road. He made an assignation with them for a later meeting and then started off back through the churchyard. Here he met two more women: his description of them is worth quoting, as an example of his style:

> They were tall, stout and dusty, had very short petti-
> coats, and thick, hob-nailed boots, dark-blue dresses
> hung over big haunches, little black shawls no larger
> than handkerchiefs over their backs. They had big
> black bonnets cocked right upon the tops of their
> heads, and seemed women who worked out of doors,
> agricultural labourers perhaps, or perhaps the wives of
> bargemen, for there was a canal through the village.
> They had the strong steady walk and the body well bal-

anced from the hips that you see in women engaged in out-door occupations; perhaps they carried straw-berries to the London markets in large baskets on their heads, and they walked as firmly as soldiers.

Walter had them, one after the other, down among the tombstones. 'There we were laying in copulation, with the dead all around us; another living creature might that moment have been begotten, in its turn to eat, drink, die, be buried and rot.' Then they went off 'with their steady step. I went to my mother's. I found I had torn a hole in the knee of my trousers.'

I started to think of possible locations for this house in the London suburbs. Camberwell was a possibility. It was within reasonable reach of a 'neighbouring great school or college' at Dulwich. The Grand Surrey Canal ran through the parish. The parish church had a very large churchyard. The route to central London was down the Waterloo Road and over Waterloo Bridge. At one period Walter was regularly walking into the centre, for he had a job of some kind at (apparently) the War Office, while waiting for the purchase of a commission to come through. If he was walking from Camberwell it would explain why, in the same period, he was frequenting the prostitutes in Granby Street, which is off Waterloo Road.

I own a copy of Stanford's large-scale plan of London, published in four sheets in the early 1860s. I looked at Camberwell on it. It showed the large churchyard of St Giles's Church, and across Camberwell Grove from it a narrow lane leading through fields and gardens – good for 'lovers on summer nights' – to Denmark Hill. In Camberwell Grove was a 'Collegiate School'. Where the lane joined Denmark Hill was a terrace of houses – De Crespigny Terrace – as described by Walter. The lane had a name, in small print difficult to read. I looked carefully. It was Love Lane. Eureka!

I went out to Camberwell to see what was on the ground today. De Crespigny Terrace is still there, though no longer so named, but numbered in with Denmark Hill. I walked along Love Lane, still so called, though metalled now and lined with later houses, crossed Camberwell Grove, and followed the route through the large disused churchyard of St Giles – separated off now by railings – to Camberwell Church Street.

De Crespigny Terrace is made up of agreeably modest detached or semi-detached classical houses, stuccoed white. Stylistically they could well have been built in the early 1830s, which would fit in with the Walter story. He was aged about sixteen when the family moved into their suburban house, and circumstantial evidence in the *Secret Life* makes it unlikely that he was born much later than 1815.

The corner house on Love Lane is, to judge from the exterior, of eight rooms, two main rooms on each floor, as Walter described his own house. I looked at it with the triumph of an explorer or a detective. Should I ring the bell, and tell whoever answered it 'Do you know that Walter, the Victorian Casanova, lived here? That it was in your second floor back that, aged 16, he made love to Charlotte, the pretty parlourmaid, the first of his 1200 women?'

I looked at the entries for Denmark Hill in the 1841 census, the first to be held in this country. They did not make clear the exact position of the houses on it, but I was intrigued by one household listed – from my point of view the only hopeful one in the census: Anna Horner, aged 65; Frances Horner, aged 30; James, aged 25; and three female servants. More research expanded Anna Horner into Anne Maria Horner, and James into her son, James Thomas Horner. Could he conceivably have been Walter, on a visit to his mother?

I worked away at the Horners and established a sizeable family tree for them. James Thomas's father, James Horner, was a wholesale chemist, of a Yorkshire family with a business in Bucklesbury in the City of London, and a big house in ample grounds on Grove Hill, Camberwell; he died in 1836. He was not quite the man of private means I had been looking for, but he had a partner and could conceivably have left the business to him, lived too expensively, and got into difficulties. His wife was born Anne Maria Bayly; there were Baylys in Jamaica, which could have explained the plantations he went out to visit, though I could not establish the connection.

Further research in the local history library in Southwark produced a detailed plan of Camberwell in 1842. I looked for De Crespigny Terrace on it. There was no sign of it; it had not been built. The house in which I had so excitedly placed Walter in the early 1830s did not then exist – was not, as I later established, built until about 1845. My house of cards collapsed.

This was a blow. But there were still plenty of other biographical details scattered through the text which were worth following up, in the hopes of their leading to an identification.

His two marriages did not seem hopeful. His first took place when he was 26. When he had come of age he got control of money left to him by his godfather, a former surgeon-major in the army. He gave up the idea of taking a commission and spent the next few years spending his legacy. The marriage may have been for money; at any rate it was a disaster: 'I hated her while I fucked her.' He spent much time narrating his grievances to sympathetic prostitutes but does not reveal the reasons for his hatred in his diary. Release came after a good few years, when he was in Paris. 'Death had done its work. Hurrah!' Then came 'four years of freedom', followed by remarriage, this time for love. 'I loved deeply, truly shall love to my dying hour.' Even so, it was not long before he had to admit that 'I have yielded – Alas – Alas – I am whoring as of old.' But no clues are given as to the identity or background of either wife.

His relationship with his aunt, and her son, his cousin Fred, seemed more helpful. Fred was important in Walter's life. He was his first fount of sexual experience, and for years the two were companions in dissipation. He went into the army, served in India and Canada, and when in London had smart, rakish friends, including Lord A - - - , who lived with his mistress in B - t - n street and who once kicked his valet and was sued by him for assault. Fred's mother, widowed early in the diary, lived on a country estate with woods, fishing, gamekeepers, a home farm and at least one tenanted farm. If the initials were to be relied on, it was in Hertfordshire. There was a paper mill nearby. The grounds or park contained several ornamental features, including a sizeable summerhouse or grotto, built of rockwork but with a roof partly of timber; the roof was in decay, enabling Walter to climb up and peer through a gap in it to watch his 14-year-old cousin Joe ('whose nursemaid years before I had shagged') making love to the parlourmaid.

Another possibly identifiable relative was an uncle in the North, about two miles from 'D - - l - - g - - n' which could only be Darlington. He was married with children and lived with his wife on a sizeable estate which mainly belonged to her, in an old-built house in beautiful grounds, at the end of a 'quiet village'.

Walter had an 'intimate friend' who had been the defending counsel in a case which got much publicity at the time. It concerned the wife of a printer, who used to come back late at night from his work at a daily newspaper. His wife would leave the door on the latch for him. A fellow-lodger took advantage of this to get into her bed and make love to her when she was half-asleep and thought it was her husband. She subsequently gave him on charge for rape. But was it rape when she had not resisted?

Other friends included: an old schoolfellow, now a very

wealthy merchant, living at B - - - f - - d, probably Bradford; a large ship owner with whom he visited the docks in London; one of the largest dyers and skinners in Glasgow; a boyhood friend and neighbour whose father was a gun manufacturer in the East End; a sculptor who drank himself to death, and a painter who was still alive.

I worked away at all of these. It would be wearisome to go in any detail into my work in libraries, on the computer and in the National Archives, my trawling through Post Office directories, wills and censures, my search for likely grottoes or suitable landowners in the Darlington neighbourhood. Most of my research got nowhere, or at best led to an intriguing trail which suddenly died on me or proved false. The alcoholic sculptor might have been the Cornishman Neville Northey Burnard, who was taken up in London in the 1840s and '50s but returned to Cornwall to die in the workhouse at Redruth in 1878; or the Yorkshire man Joseph Bentley Leyland, who had a similar but shorter London vogue and then retreated back to Yorkshire, where he and Branwell Bronte made friends, got drunk together and both died young; but I could find out nothing about other friends of either man. I ran to earth references of three rape cases of the type in which Walter's barrister friend was involved, but when I looked into these they took place in circumstances different from those described by Walter. I could not locate any grotto with an appropriate family attached to it.

I kept thinking of Camberwell, with its Love Lane and churchyard. A possible theory occurred to me. Might it be that Walter's *My Secret Life* was like George Borrow's *Lavengro*? This is a mixture of genuine memories and fabrication which no one has been able to disentangle. Could adventures in *My Secret Life* have indeed happened to Walter, but at different times and in different circumstances from those described by him? Was he on occasions taking actual places known to him and filling them with invention? It at least seemed worth discovering who actually occupied that corner house in De Crespigny Terrace when it was first built in about 1844–45.

This, the census and rates revealed to me, was Richard Robert Roberts, living with his wife Catherine, born (according to the 1851 census) in about 1805, and too old to make a convincing Walter. But living a few doors away, in the biggest house in the Terrace, was my old discarded candidate James Thomas Horner, no longer in the house of his mother (she had died in 1843) but now an independent householder. And, oddly enough, when Horner moved out of De Crespigny Terrace in 1849 or 1850, Roberts left his own house and moved in – possibly a purely commercial transaction, but also suggesting the possibility of a friendship between the two men.

His unexpected reappearance shook me. Could I have been on the right track after all? I did a little more work on him. When he left De Crespigny Terrace I lost track of him for a few years, but in the 1861 census he was living on Herne Hill, described as a 'drug merchant', along with his wife Mary, his niece Eliza Pearson and six servants. In the 1870s he retired and moved to Nobright, a substantial house at Godstone in Kent, with its own lodge and possibly its own farm. Here he died in 1889, worth £68,000.

According to Walter's editor, if there was such a person, Walter gave him the manuscript of the *Diary* two years before his death. It was three years before he looked at it, and then a few years before he edited it for publication. He claims to have been his friend at school and college and the executor of his will, and says that his wife died a year after him and that he had no family.

J. T. Horner also seems to have had no family, or at least no children, for he left everything outright to his wife, with no mention of anyone else. But she was still alive in 1899; his executor (jointly with her), Henry Seymour Beresford Webb, was a much younger man, possibly a relative, for later he was the occupant and presumably owner of the house. He was the author of a Spanish grammar and other textbooks. This does not fit in with the circumstances of publication as described in the *Diary*, but then this description may have been deliberately concocted to confuse the story. It is at least possible that, just as the personality of the jovial British businessman in John Buchan's *The Thirty-Nine Steps* was peeled away to reveal a German master-spy, so behind James Thomas Horner, wholesale chemist, lurked Walter, the great erotomane. But it does not seem too likely, and I certainly have not proved it. I fear that Horner was exactly what he seemed to be – a respectable, respectably married and modestly affluent City businessman.

It was at about this stage that I gave up. I had already wasted more time on Walter than he was worth. It was time to move on to more serious projects, too long delayed. I left him with little regret, though still modest curiosity; it may be that one of these days I will accidentally come across the key to the identity or that others, perhaps intrigued by this essay, may find it. Meanwhile, goodbye Walter. I know, if your own account is to be relied on, how you lived; I mildly wonder how you died. You expressed your own hopes in your diary:

Since we all must die some time, let us pray to die in the ecstasy of obeying the divine law that draws men and women together in carnal union. But I wonder how many men are fortunate to depart in this supreme pleasure.

6
Drooling Victorians:
the strange story of Pet Marjorie

A MONG THE CURIOSITIES of biographical dictionaries
the pseudonymous Walter can be matched with Marjory
Fleming, the only eight-year-old in the *DNB*. I owe my
knowledge of her to a chance pick-up in the local Oxfam
bookshop: *The Complete Marjory Fleming: her Journals,
Letters and Verses*, transcribed and edited by Frank Sidgwick,
1934. Below the title on the dust-cover was a quotation from
Robert Louis Stevenson: 'Marjory Fleming was possibly – no,
I take back possibly – she was one of the noblest works of
God.' On opening the book and discovering that she had died
of measles in 1811, shortly before her ninth birthday, I was
sufficiently intrigued to buy it.

Marjory Fleming was born in Kirkcaldy, Fifeshire, in
1803. Her father was a Kirkcaldy accountant, her mother
came from a family of Edinburgh surgeons who were friends
of, or at least friendly with, Sir Walter Scott. Her journals,
poems and letters were kept by her family, but remained
unknown until a London journalist, H. B. Farnie, came across
them and wrote an article on her, which was published in
1853 as a booklet entitled *Pet Marjorie: a Story of Child Life
Fifty Years Ago*. He claimed, without justification, that 'Pet
Marjorie' was what she was called by her family.

Farnie's pamphlet would have sunk without trace if it had
not been unexpectedly written about by Dr John Brown in the
North British Review in 1863. His article was turned into a
book, *Marjorie Fleming: a Sketch*, and became a bestseller.

His sentimental account of a bull-terrier, *Rab and his Friends,* had been another bestseller when it was published in 1861, so an expectant public was ready to take 'Pet Marjorie' to its heart. Brown gave his readers everything they could wish for about this 'warm, rosy, little wifie'. The existence of an inscribed copy of Maria Edgeworth's *Rosamund* and *Harry and Lucy* given to her by Walter Scott encouraged him to invent several pages of nauseating twaddle about the two of them: 'Marjorie! Marjorie!' shouted her friend, 'where are ye, my bonnie wee croodlin doo,' and so on. He quoted copiously from her work, not hesitating to, in his view, improve it where necessary, and provided the essential end, a tear-jerking death-bed.

It was Brown's presentation that elicited Stevenson's praise, and got Marjorie a mention in a poem by Swinburne and a tribute from Mark Twain: 'she was made out of thunderstorms and sunshine'. In 1889 Leslie Stephen, Virginia Woolf's father and a formidable person in his own right, gave her an entry in the *Dictionary of National Biography*, which he edited, and wrote it himself. A full-scale biography by Lachlan Macbean, with many illustrations, followed in 1904, and was reprinted in 1905, 1914 and 1928. For some years Marjory's house in Kirkcaldy was opened as a museum dedicated to her. In 1930 her manuscripts were presented to the National Library of Scotland. A collotype facsimile of them, edited by Arundell Esdaile, was published shortly after. Frank Sidgwick's book followed in 1934, complete with introduction, family tree, copious notes, appendices and index.

And what are her writings like? They are charming, especially as presented by Sidgwick in a typescript version of the manuscript, complete with wide spacing, crossings out and corrections. Her lessons, naughtinesses, friendships, readings and all the events of each day, along with pious reflections and maxims evoked by her Presbyterian family, are mixed up together and expressed in language half-grown up and half-childish. A couple of quotations may give their flavour:

> I am now going to tell you about the horrible and wretched plaege that my multiplication gives me you cant conceive it – the most Devilish thing is 8 times 8 & 7 times 7 is what nature itself cant endure.

> I confess that I have been more like a little young Devil than a creature for when Isabella went up the stairs to teach me religion and my multiplication and to be good and all my other lessons I stamped with my feet and threw my new hat which she made on the ground and was sulky and was dreadfully passionate . . .

Her prose is much better than her verse, of which one of the few good couplets can suffice. They start off a poem on her pet monkey:

> O lovely O most charming pug
> Thy gracefull air and heavenly mug.

But to call her, as Macbean does, a child genius is ridiculous. She is no better or more delightful than other precocious children of character, writing or drawing before self-consciousness sets in to destroy their directness.

Most of the publications on her include a watercolour portrait by her cousin and patient teacher, Isabella. It is hard to read her character from this as Dr John Brown did: 'looking straight at us – fearless and full of love, passionate, wild, willful, fancy's child'. She looks a tough little nut, but none the worse for that.

Having looked up what Leslie Stephen had to say on her in the *DNB*, I was naturally intrigued to see whether she had made it to the new *ODNB*. So I went to the London Library to check and there she was, with her portrait reproduced this time, and a new entry:

> The general revaluation of juvenile and adult perception of childhood has led in the 1990s to a new consideration of Marjory as a socially situated early nineteenth-century child and Victorian mythic appropriation. Her status seems assured.

7
The wrong castle: a Charlotte Mew correction

I THINK I FIRST came to Charlotte Mew by way of Penelope Fitzgerald's biography of her. This got me interested in
the minuscule lesbian poet, with her alternation of wild
fooling and rigid conventionality, her failed architect father
who had married above him, her life of shabby gentility in
increasingly shrinking Bloomsbury residences, with a beloved
sister and a silly demanding mother, all three trying to conceal
the fact that they had to take in lodgers to make ends meet,
her fear of the insanity in her family (an uncle living with a
carer, a sister and brother in asylums), her hopeless crushes on
unresponsive women, her ultimate distress at the death of her
sister, followed by her suicide, possibly committed in the fear
that she herself was going mad.

But above all the biography led me to the poems. I had not
known or even heard of them. They were a discovery that
gave me several months of excitement. I took out of the
London Library the first edition of the first of her two
volumes of poems, *The Farmer's Bride*. It was published by
the Poetry Bookshop in 1916 and is evocative, with its coarse
hand-made paper and cover design of a rather arts-and-crafty
farmhouse by Lovat Fraser, of the seriousness and excitement
of sessions in the little room up the steep stair from the Bookshop in which poets read their own poems and the poems of
others, and in which Charlotte Mew made her first public
appearance, coming up the stairs into the room to an audi-

ence amazed by the odd, tiny figure, who said, apologetically, 'Yes, I'm afraid it's me.'

Mew writes – sometimes in short lyrics, sometimes in longer poems of broken, irregularly rhyming verse – about broken, incomplete, unhappy or frustrated people. In the best of them she writes with the immediacy of someone who felt damaged herself. One of the best, and best known, of her poems is 'Ken'. This concerns a mentally handicapped and physically repellent 'Ken' whom the 'I' of the poem encounters in a small country town:

> When first I came upon him there
> Suddenly, on the half-lit stair,
> I think I hardly found a trace
> Of likeness to a human face
> In his. And I said then
> If in His image God made men
> Some other must have made poor Ken –
> But for his eyes which looked at you
> As two red, wounded stars might do.
>
> He scarcely spoke, you scarcely hear
> His voice broke off in little jars,
> To tears sometimes. An uncouth bird
> He seemed as he ploughed up the street,
> Groping, with knarred, high-lifted feet
> And arms thrust out as if to beat
> Always against a threat of bars.
> And oftener than not there'd be
> A child just higher than his knee
> Trotting beside him . . .

The poem ends with his removal to an asylum:

> So, when they took
> Ken to that place, I did not look

> After he called and turned on me
> His eyes. These I shall see –

In her biography, Penelope Fitzgerald suggests that the town in which Ken lives, described as containing a big church and a castle, is inspired by Carisbrooke in the Isle of Wight, the island from which the Mew family originated. But the descriptions in the poem make it clear that it is not Carisbrooke, but Arundel in Sussex.

The poem describes a Catholic, or part-Catholic, town; the church which dominates it is a Catholic church; it has a castle and a deer park:

> The town is old and very steep
> A place of bells and cloisters and grey towers,
> And black clad people walking in their sleep –
> A nun, a priest, a woman taking flowers
> To her new grave; and watched from end to end
> By the great Church above . . .

Ken liked to go to church and

>   . . . used to fix
> His eyes upon a crucifix
> In a dark corner . . .
> You did not look at him as he sat there,
> Biting his rosary to bits.
> While pointing to the Christ he tried to say,
> 'Take it away.' . . .

> The children wake to dart from doors and call
> Down the wide, crooked street, where, at the bend,
> Before it climbs up to the park,
> Ken's is the gabled house facing the Castle wall.

>   . . . Through his dim
> Long twilight this, at least, shone clear,

That all the children and the deer,
Whom every day he went to see
Out in the park, belonged to him.

Arundel, unlike Carisbrooke (no great Catholic church, no nuns, no deer park) is the one town in England which fits this description. It is a hill town, dominated by the 'grey towers' of the castle and, even higher, by the hill-top silhouette of the great church of St Philip Neri (in recent decades promoted to be the Catholic Cathedral), built by the 15th Duke of Norfolk in 1869–73. The great crucifix is still there, in a 'dark corner' in the South transept. The 'wide crooked street' is clearly the High Street which, in its upper half, climbs up beside the castle wall, past the former St Wilfred's Convent, and then changes direction to go on up to the lodge gates, giving access to the deer park – passing the graveyard of the parish church and the new Catholic cemetery on the way. The house where Ken lived, 'at the bend' and 'facing the castle wall' is clearly recognisable as either what is now called Sefton House, a seventeeth- and eighteenth-century casing of a medieval framework, or its neighbour, now known as Chester House, a Victorian building with a gabled, pseudo-half-timbered upper storey.

Charlotte Mew's poems are not necessarily autobiographical, but some are certainly inspired by incidents in her life. There is no record of her going to Arundel, or having friends there, but this does not mean much, as her biography is sparsely documented and full of gaps. She had, however, a grandmother, an aunt and an uncle living in Brighton, from which Arundel was easily accessible by train. When her grandmother died her aunt left Brighton but her brother stayed on in lodgings with a carer; he was in some way handicapped, though not, it seems likely, to the extent of 'Ken'.

In Arundel there was, in fact, a severely handicapped resident in the 1880s and 1890s. This was the Earl of Arundel, the son and heir of the Duke of Norfolk, born in 1879. He was mentally retarded and born epileptic and blind. His mother died when he was eight, leaving him alone with his father in the castle; it was said that 'no father could have loved the most attractive and perfect child more than he did his afflicted one'. He died in 1902, aged 22. It is possible that Charlotte Mew's poem could have been inspired by a visit to Arundel, and by seeing or just hearing of Lord Arundel, who was a familiar sight in the town being taken for an airing with his nurse or attendant in a pony cart. He may even have attended Mass in the new church.

And yet there is a vividness and precision about her description of Ken and his activities which suggests an actual person, and that person much less grand than poor Lord Arundel who, in spite of his disabilities, was treated with the deference due to his birth (he retired from Arundel a few years before he died to his own household and butler in Ascot).

Anyway, it seemed at least worth looking at the census returns, to see who lived in Sefton and Chester Houses, at the relevant, or likely to be relevant, date. This must have been before 1913, when the poem was first published; but it could be well before this, for Mew certainly stored up memories and re-used them at a later date.

The ownership histories of Sefton House did not sound very promising: lived in from at least 1895 till about 1905 by George H. Bulbeck, a timber-merchant, and by his son who was in the family business, then empty for a few years, then from about 1908 occupied by a local brewer, Guy Constable. Chester House was a little more promising. From at least 1891 it was occupied by George T. Evershed, described as a 'soap manufacturer'. He lived there with his wife, son and three daughters, the middle one of whom, Alice, was born in 1870, the year after Charlotte Mew. So they could have been friends; but of course there is no obvious reason why they should have been, unless one can find a connection.

There is, in fact, a possible one in the form of George T. Evershed's brother, Arthur. From 1873 to 1894 he was a doctor in Hampstead, living with his wife and seven children, born from 1865 onwards. In 1882, for eighteen months or so, Charlotte was walking every day from Bloomsbury to Hampstead for English lessons from Lucy Harrison, the former headmistress of Gower Street School, where she had been educated. Lucy Harrison had had some kind of breakdown or crisis, as a result of which she had temporarily left the school, but continued to teach in Hampstead. This is certainly not a proved connection, but at least suggests a possible route which could have led Charlotte, by way of Evershed fellow-pupils in Hampstead, to their cousins in Arundel.

But what about Ken himself? There is no one recognisable as him in Sefton or Chester Houses in the census returns of 1891, 1901 or 1911 which, if correctly filled in, should identify people who were not of whole mind. But again there is a possibility in the third of the three Evershed brothers, Charles Lambert Evershed. He was a qualified surgeon, and also medical officer to the East Preston Union – that is to say, a public servant concerned with the welfare of the poor, in so far as there was any public service to the poor in those days.

The great monument or mausoleum of poverty in the Arundel area was the formidable East Preston Workshouse, rebuilt on a massive scale in 1872–73. Like other workhouses, it also served as a hospital and mental asylum for paupers. Its long bleak facade would have loured down on Charlotte Mew if and when she travelled by rail from

Brighton to Arundel. It came close enough to the 'red brick barn upon the hill' with its 'twenty windows in a row' to which Ken was consigned.

C. L. Evershed lived and had his consulting room in Arundel. In 1881 he was living half-way along Maltravers Street, the long street that goes out of the High Street by Chester House. In 1891 he had moved both consulting room and residence to a house on the High Street, a few doors down from Chester House. In the Post Office directory of 1895 his address is given as Maltravers Street, with no indications as to whereabouts; there were still no street numbers in Arundel.

Chester House consists in fact of two sections, both with the same distinctive architecture, the main portion in front, and a wing at the back with a separate entrance door on Maltravers Street. Could it have been here that C. L. Evershed was living in 1895? Could he, for treatment or charity, have taken in from the East Preston Workhouse someone resembling Ken, who had to go back to the workhouse, perhaps, when Evershed died in 1898?

This is a possible scenario, but no more than that. Perhaps some day some solid documentation to prove the theory right or wrong will be found, to establish just what it was that took Charlotte Mew walking up the High Street in Arundel, and who it was she saw there.

8

Horrors made harmless:
Masefield and *The Midnight Folk*

JOHN MASEFIELD once told a friend that *The Midnight Folk* was his favourite book. I can understand why; I fell in love with it, and to a lesser extent with its sequel *The Box of Delights*, when I was first introduced to them at my preparatory school, and am still fond of them over sixty years later. In recent years I have found that when I am having difficulty in getting to sleep, to move in my imagination into the world of *The Midnight Folk* can drive away disturbing worries and fantasies and bring on sleep, almost infallibly. It is odd, perhaps, that an unassuming children's book should have this therapeutic effect; but I suspect that writing it was therapeutic for John Masefield himself, and that that is why he was fond of it.

The two books both centre on the adventures of 'little Kay Harker', but are different in character. Both were written for Masefield's children, but *The Box of Delights* (1935) was written eight years later, when they were teenagers, and his daughter was old enough to provide it with naifly charming illustrations. Although *The Midnight Folk* (1927) is set in the 1880s or thereabouts, for *The Box of Delights*, perhaps at his children's request, Masefield coolly moved the setting forty or fifty years on and made it contemporary, though the main characters remained the same. The 1880s were the years of Masefield's own childhood (he was born in 1878), and *The Midnight Folk* is much more closely related to it.

It tells the story of a nine- or ten-year old orphan living in a sizeable house under the care of an unsympathetic governess and, at long distance, a pompous guardian. He is trying to find and return to its rightful owners the treasure of a South American cathedral which his great-grandfather, a sea-captain, had taken on board his ship to save from revolutionary troops but had lost when the crew mutinied, set him ashore and sailed off; they were subsequently shipwrecked, and the treasure never seen again. Kay's allies in the search are a variety of animals and humans; his enemies are a coven of witches and a sinister rosy-cheeked American magician, Abner Brown. They are trying to find the treasure for themselves. The book is thick with magic, good and bad; after a crowded week of excitement the treasure is found and returned to its rightful owners.

The book is by no means straightforwardly autobiographical. Most obviously, Kay Harker is an only child, whereas Masefield was one of a family of six. But by and large the setting is the Herefordshire landscape and townscape of Masefield's childhood, in which he lived, as he later wrote, in paradise up till the age of six and a half and, in spite of some griefs, with much happiness after that. To write the book, he went joyfully back to these years, but spun out of them something related but different, a world in which dream merges into reality, portraits come alive, animals speak, Kay himself shrinks or becomes invisible or flies through the air, and yet this world is filled with delightful and far from dream-like characters, Kay included. Moreover, into its golden glow he dips whatever was unhappy or painful in his childhood or boyhood: his loss of his mother, his hatred of his governess, the stories that scared or haunted him, his fear of the dark, the traumas that he suffered at sea, and these are transformed and made harmless.

Following on Masefield's early loss of his mother and father, his childhood was dominated by his governess. He loathed her so much that he once went for her with a fork and tried to kill her. This incident much impressed Yeats when Masefield told him of it; he used to enjoy introducing the gentle and charming Masefield as 'my murderer'.

A governess features prominently in *The Midnight Folk*, and is clearly related to Masefield's. She has no fondness for Kay, is clearly bored and resentful at having to look after a little boy, and she is always telling him off. As Kay is a delightful and interesting child, it is exasperating for the reader to read of her failure to appreciate him. But Masefield, who could so easily have got his own back in a vicious portrait, treats her not without sympathy. Kay endures her, rather than hates her. She plays the piano well, and sings to it with a voice so beautiful that Kay, in bed in the room above, is 'rapt away into joy'; she draws 'rather well', too. She gets her final come-uppance not by being stuck with a fork, but by being unmasked as Sylvia Daisy Pouncer, the chief of the witches. But she walks out of the story unscathed, to reappear in *The Box of Delights*, married to Abner Brown and running with him a centre for gangsters and burglars, disguised as a theological seminary.

In Masefield's account of his childhood in *So Long to Learn* (1952), his governess has been censored out altogether. The childhood chapter of the book includes only one upsetting incident. When he was aged eight, a long-locked cupboard was opened by an uncle to reveal piles of old magazines, which the uncle dismisssed as rubbish and said should be thrown away. The other grown-ups were equally scornful, but 'while they were busy I looked deeper into the piles, and saw, deep down, well-covered, the serial issues of a story with the most frightful illustrations'. While the magazines were lying undisturbed, waiting to be burned, he managed to abstract these issues and carry them to his secret hiding-place. This was under the bed in the best bedroom, where the valances of the bed made a kind of cave. By turning up a flap of carpet he could make 'a hiding place within the hiding place', and in this he placed the magazines and their story. 'For terrifying horror, at the age of eight, it was all, and more than all, the heart's desire. I will not say what it was. Each issue was shocking: and each was headed by a coarse and vigorous illustration of a horror beyond my dreams, beyond my nightmares. I enjoyed creeping to my tepee and tasting these horrors' – not after dark, though, when the horror was too great. But one day he crawled in for another taste of the story, and the magazines had gone – perhaps, as he later surmised, found and removed by a cleaning housemaid 'who may have thought they had lain there for years'.

Pornographic? Sadistic? Whatever the story was, it was perhaps the after-effects of reading it that is referred to in his poem 'The Death Rooms', in which he wrote about the time of his marriage in 1903:

> My soul has many an old decaying room
> Hung with the ragged arras of the past.
> Where startled faces flicker in the gloom
> And horrid whispers set the cheek aghast . . .
>
> None dwells in these old rooms: none ever can –
> I pass them through at night with hidden head;
> Lock'd rotting rooms her eyes must never scan,
> Floors that her blessed feet must never tread.

In *The Midnight Folk* the secret hiding place reappears, though not behind the bed valances in the best bedroom, but behind those of the dressing table in Kay's own room. It also has its 'hiding place within a hiding place' under the carpet, and in it Kay places a book which he discovers by chance, purloins, and crawls into his hidey-hole to read. But there is nothing in the least terrifying or horrible about the book and its contents. It was among those which Roper Bilges, the unattractive gamekeeper of a neighbouring landowner, had found in his grandfather's old sea chest and thrown out. The book itself was a manual entitled *The Sea Gunner's Practice*, by B. Blastem, Master Gunner, but although Kay was intrigued by sections headed 'To make the fine mealed Gun-Powder for Priming' and 'To make Coloured Flares and other Artificial Fire Works', what really interested him about it was that the flyleaf was inscribed with the name of his great-grandfather, 'Aston Harker, Seekings House, 1804' and above all that what had been a section of empty pages for notes, at the end, had been filled in crude handwriting with 'The true statement of Roper Bilges, gunner in the ship *Plunderer*, Captain Harker, master.' In this Bilges described how he had led the mutineers who seized control of the ship and its treasure, but how he himself had been seized in his turn by Twiney Pricker, the ship's sailmaker, who came in the night with 'Jake and the coffin-maker and English Joe, that deserted the Blanche frigate, and had her on his stomach in blue', saying '. . . we'll no more Bilges for captain,' and marooned him ashore just as the mutineers had previously marooned Captain Harker. The discovery of this account was all part of the search which helped Kay to piece together the history and ultimate fate of the treasure.

Another period of Masefield's life that appears, curiously transformed, in *The Midnight Folk* is the time he spent at sea. Although it was not till the publication of his verse stories *The Everlasting Mercy* and *The Widow in the Bye Streeet* in 1911 and 1912 that he acquired and kept the, for poetry, huge sales that made him a prewar equivalent to John Betjeman and similarly led him to the Laureateship, his reputation as a poet was established by his first volume of poetry, *Salt-Water Ballads*, published in 1902. This contained his two most anthologised poems, 'Sea Cargoes' and 'Sea Fever'. 'Sea Cargoes' ('Quinquireme of Nineveh from distant Ophir', etc.) I first read at my preparatory school, as printed, with accompanying woodcuts, in *The Dragon Book of Verse*. The same anthology also included 'Sea Fever', but I got to know this especially well when, as hauntingly set to music by John Ireland, it was my house's entry in the inter-house Singing Competition at Ampleforth in 1945 or 1946. According to the rules of the competition, every member of each house had to take part but, as my singing voice was not deemed an attractive one, I was placed inconspicuously in the centre of the house group and ordered to open and shut my mouth but let no sound come out. Even so, words and tune are still engrained in my memory:

> I must go down to the seas again
> To the lonely seas and the sky
> And all I ask is a tall ship
> And a star to steer it by . . . etc.

Reading these and other early poems left me with a vague idea that Masefield was a kind of English Conrad, though with a background of sail, not steam. In fact his entire sailing experience lasted only four months, from April till August 1894, when he was aged 15 to 16. Far from 'running away to sea', as the literary gossip about him later went, he owed this part of his career to his unattractively dominating aunt, who had decided that he was too soft, and that a career at sea would 'make a man of him'. He was accordingly sent for two years' training in HMS *Conway*, a former sailing ship permanently anchored in the Mersey by Liverpool as a Merchant Service training ship. From this he went on in 1894 to serve as an apprentice in a four-masted barque, *The Gilcruix*, belonging to the White Star Line. This set out from Cardiff at the end of April, carrying a cargo of compressed coal-dust blocks and bound for Iquique, in Chile.

Apart from a brief but violent squall south of Rio de Janeiro, the journey was uneventful until the ship reached Cape Horn. Then followed, as Masefield later wrote, 'thirty-two days of such storm and cold as I hope never to see again . . . Seas forty foot high and two miles long, and ice everywhere, on deck, in the rigging, and tumbling in the sea, and we fighting the lot of it' or, as he wrote in his poem 'Doubt' (1913):

> Soul, body, brain
> Knew nothing but the wind, the cold, the pain.

But finally the battered ship emerged into calm waters, and limped up the South American coast to Iquique. This was the end of Masefield's sailing career. He had some kind of collapse, was invalided out of the ship's crew, and the ship sailed off without him. After a few weeks in hospital in Valparaiso, he was returned in slow stages to England.

On his return his aunt mocked him for having 'failed to stick it', and sent him back to sea as soon as possible. A berth as an apprentice was found for him on another four-masted barque, the *Bidston Hill*. As the ship was in New York, he was sent out as a passenger by steamship to join it, but deserted before the ship left harbour. After a few weeks as a vagrant, he found work, first in an Irish bar and then in a carpet factory at Yonkers, just outside New York. From this he finally returned to England, working his way there as a steerage steward on a passenger steamship.

Once back, he never showed the slightest sign of a compulsion to 'go down to the seas again'. His sea poems were written eight or more years later, securely on dry land in London and elsewhere; and for the rest of his long life he made his home as far from the sea as possible.

A sea voyage is among the adventures featured in *The Midnight Folk*, but it is far removed from the horrors of Masefield's sail round the Horn. It is all pure joy. It takes place in the model of Captain Harker's ship, the *Plunderer*, which hangs in Kay's room and in the magical hours of the night is carried to Kay's bedside by the waters which swirl out from the brook in a hunting print on the wall. It is captained by Kay's friend the Water Rat, and the crew consists of tiny water mice; but Kay is miraculously tiny, too. The ship, with Kay comfortable and cosseted aboard, sails out of the window, down the stream in the garden to the river, and down the river to 'open sea, out of sight of land, with the ship under full sail flying westward . . . The sea was all blue and bright, the hot sun was shining, not a cloud could be seen. The ship was flying faster and faster.'

It finally anchors in calm water 'not far from a low, tropical shore, blindingly white, from the surf bursting on it.' It is immediately over the wreck of the real *Plunderer*. Kay descends in a diving bell, and four 'young and merry-looking mermaids' usher him out to the sea bed, and show him the wreck of the ship and one surviving gold figure from the treasure 'lying among the coral, as though he were resting upon a bank of flowers'.

> All the floor of the sea shone. At first he thought that everything there was dead; but when he had been twenty seconds in that tingling water, he knew that it was full of life . . . All those living forms were swaying gently, as the swell lifted and fell: all were glistening and tingling with joy; a kind of drowsy song of delight moved through the water, everything was singing, or murmuring, or sighing, because life was so good.

After some frolicking with the mermaids, Kay rejoins the ship, now sailing for home, and finds himself sitting on the end of the *Plunderer*'s jib-boom in the clouds of spray flung up as she sailed: 'Then he saw that it was not spray, but a flight of flying fish skimming and falling like darts, all glittering and quivering. "Oh, how lovely," he cried – but then he was back in his bed.'

The sensation of flying, as the ship in full sail flew westward, or as Kay sat on the jib-boom on his return, is repeated in flights through the air throughout the book: on broomsticks purloined from the witches with Nibbins the cat, flying with bats' wings provided by his friend Bat to visit Tom Otter in his watery home, flying in seven-league boots to rescue Nibbins and Bitem, the fox, when they are trapped in a cave. But the most memorable of the flights is with a 'somewhat fierce but smiling lady', on a winged black horse, who mysteriously watches over Kay, and when Mrs Pouncer is conjuring up spirits to give her information about the whereabouts of the treasure, rides uninvited into her magic circle and defies her. Soon after, '"Kay," said a sweet voice at the window', and Kay finds the same lady on her horse, treading air outside his bedroom, and is invited: 'Won't you come and ride with me?' They soar off, first to feed the four weathercocks on the four pinnacles of the church tower with golden corn from the horse's nosebag, then to fly north at great speed through the summer night, and finally to coast down to a moonlit lake and a great house, and dismount at its one lit-up window to find a big double-bed and 'a wicked old woman in a very gay dressing-down . . . reading a sprightly story, at which she was laughing. Beside her, on a table, was a bottle of champagne.' That was Susan Pricker, alias Piney Trigger, the daughter of Twiney Pricker the sailmaker, who had emerged from his shady past as Sir Piney Trigger, Honduras merchant, of Trigger Hall, and had found the treasure and brought it to England.

The mysterious lady brings Kay back to his bed and then disappears, until the very end of the book, when the treasure has been discovered and the governess has gone. Kay is told that someone is waiting for him in the drawing-room, goes down apprehensively, and is amazed to find her standing by the fireplace, and to be told by her: 'I am Caroline Louisa, who loved your mother. I could not come before, but now I am going to live here and look after you.' They are playing cricket in the garden together when the Archbishop and the Dictator of Santa Barbara arrive to collect the treasure.

But Caroline Louisa was the name of John Masefield's mother. Masefield was reticent about his mother, who died when he was aged six and a half and whom he barely remembered, but whom he seems to have recreated in his mind in idealised form. He wrote one sad short poem, 'To C. L.', and it must be to her death that he is referring in his *So Long to Learn*, when he writes that his life in Paradise as a little child was shattered by 'certain happenings'. Her appearance in *The Midnight Folk*, first as a kind of magical guardian angel, then transformed into a down-to-earth guardian (as which she reappears in *The Box of Delights*) is curious, but in keeping with other transformations in the book.

Right at the beginning of *The Midnight Folk,* Kay, being led through secret passages by Nibbins the black cat, came to a little room with names carved on the wall – Robert Point-nose, Bruno Bree, Snowball, G. C. Brown Bear, and so on. Nibbins calls them 'the guards', but Kay knows the names only too well: they were those of his beloved toys, who 'had all been packed away long ago, when the governess came, because, as he had heard her tell Ellen, "they will only remind him of the past".' This sounds as though it could be auto-biographical, and relate again to the death of Masefield's mother; one is reminded of Oscar Wilde's son Vyvyan Holland writing in his autobiography about the sudden disappearance of all his toys, following on his father's trial, disgrace, bankruptcy, and the sale of all the contents of his house. If something similar happened to Masefield, in *The Midnight Folk* the toys are gloriously brought back. Like Kay, they have gone off to look for the treasure; it is they, not Kay, who finally discover it, bring it back to Seekings House, and remain there as part of the happiness expressed in the book's closing sentence: 'Nothing but peace and mirth all day long and at night peace, the owls crying, the crickets chirping and all sorts of fun going on among THE MIDNIGHT FOLK.'

9

Glossing over the seamy side:
Pepita and the Sackville-Wests

FOR SIX DAYS in February 1910 the British public could gorge itself on a deliciously juicy scandal in high life, as the newspapers reported word by word the proceedings of the Sackville peerage case. Its background was as follows. When the bachelor Lionel Sackville-West, 2nd Lord Sackville, had died in 1908, his heir appeared to be his nephew, another Lionel, the son of his deceased younger brother, William. But the elder Lionel, if was revealed in the court case, had lived for years with Josefa Duran, known as Pepita, a part-gipsy Spanish dancer, and had had a brood of illegitimate children by her. One of these, Henry, was now claiming that by the time he was born his parents were married, and that he, not the younger Lionel, was accordingly the rightful heir to the Sackville peerage, to the family estates, and to fabulous Knole, with its tapestries, silver furniture, the thousand deer in its deer park and its rumoured seven courtyards, twelve staircases and three hundred and sixty-five windows.

To add to the complications of the story, the defendant, the younger Lionel, was married to Victoria, elder sister of the plaintiff, Henry. Their daughter, Vita, was aged 18 at the time of the law suit. It must have been traumatic for her to have the family's dirty linen so very publicly washed, her mother's illegitimacy and disreputable ancestry splashed across the newspapers, and to know that if her uncle won the case her father would be dispossessed and that Knole, of which she was passionately fond, would cease to be her home.

For Henry there was one awkward obstacle to be cleared away. On 10 January 1851 Pepita had married another dancer, Juan Antonio de la Oliva, and he had remained very much alive until 1889. In spite of clumsy attempts to interfere with or falsify the parish register, Henry could not get round this marriage, and his case collapsed accordingly.

Twenty-seven years later Vita Sackville-West wrote about her grandmother and her story in her book *Pepita*. To a professional writer, as she had become, the story was irresistible, not least because it was based on a cache of unpublished material such as all historians and biographers dream about, in this case the detailed reports drawn up by the Sackville-West agents who had been sent to Spain, France and Italy to look into Pepita's background. Inevitably, the resulting book evoked snide comment about the disgracefulness of publicising one's mother's illegitimacy (just as Vita's son Nigel was to be slated in the 1970s for exposing his mother's lesbianism). But in fact *Pepita* is the best and most enjoyable of Vita Sackville-West's books, because of the warmth and strong feeling with which it is written, the colourful story that she has to tell and the skill with which it is put together. In it she came to terms with the scandal in her background by turning what could have seemed a squalid story into a romantic and moving one – something probably easier to do in the 1930s than in 1910. She revelled in the contrast between Knole and its deer park on the one hand, with generations of Dukes and Earls of Dorset, her ancestors, behind it, and the teeming, bohemian world of Spanish gipsies, dancers, old clothes-dealers, petty tradesmen, thieves and bandits, on the other, and in the fact that she was descended from both of them. Above all she fell in love with Pepita, or the image of Pepita as she recreated it on the basis of the material gathered by the family lawyers or her knowledge of her own mother who, she was convinced, resembled Pepita.

She quotes, for instance, a fellow dancer, describing Pepita in Madrid. 'She was such a striking person that once seen you could not possibly mistake her. I stood looking at her as she went down the street. I can even remember the dress she wore. She had on a dark coloured gown with the shawl known as the *manton decapucha* with many colours, and on her head she wore a black Spanish mantilla. She wore the sorbijilla, that is the lock or ring on the cheek by the ear'.

'Oh young and lovely gipsy', Vita enthuses, 'how glad I am that you once passed down a street in Madrid, before a cafe frequented by artists, so very handsome that you attracted everyone's attention in your mantilla and your manton, the sorbijilla on your cheek, and lived to work out the strange career which after many vicissitudes made you the mother of my mother . . .

'Why should I be afraid of invoking you or my own mother, who are both dead though you were both once so much alive – more vividly and troublesomely alive than most people? You both made trouble for everybody connected with you. You were both that sort of person. Yet you were both adored.'

The story as told in *Pepita* starts with a disreputable couple from Andalucia, the ex-circus girl and half-gipsy Catalina and her lover Manuel Lopez, a former cobbler and occasional bandit. They are living in a basement in Madrid and trying to make a living selling clothes from door to door. But all Catalina's love and hopes are centered on her beautiful and alluring daughter, 19-year-old Josefa, known as Pepita, whom she had trained as a dancer in Malaga, and has now brought to Madrid in the hopes of launching her in the capital. She fails, because, though all the men fall for her, Pepita is not very good at dancing. But a young professional dancer in the Madrid theatres, Juan Antonio de la Oliva, falls in love with her and marries her in January 1851. The marriage collapses after a few months, for reasons that remain obscure; her husband was later to say that the causes were 'not honourable to Pepita', but that he blamed her behaviour on her mother.

The story then moves on three years or so to the arrival of Catalina and Lopez at the village of Albolote, near Granada. They come with a French maid, to look after Catalina, a German governess, to look after Lola (Lopez's little daughter by a previous relationship), a carriage pulled by three splendid horses, a coachman and two pet dogs. They move into one of the biggest houses in the village, remodel and refurnish it, and entertain there with lavishly indiscriminate hospitality.

The reason for this rags-to-riches metamorphosis is soon revealed by Catalina, who loves to talk about it. It is 'Pepa – my little Pepa – my Pepita – my daughter the famous ballerina.' Not only does she now have engagements all over Europe, she has acquired a rich and generous protector. Hence the money pouring into Albolote. Pepita herself comes on a visit to her mother in 1855, and again in 1858. In 1855 the carriage, a band and most of the village meet her and escort her to the house, and there is a splendid ball. She is friendly to everyone, and loves showing off her jewel boxes full of jewels, and cupboards full of magnificent dresses.

By the time of the 1858 visit, the establishment has moved to a larger and grander house, out of the village in its own estate and vineyards, done up to the nines too, with a statue of Pepita dressed for dancing in the courtyard. Here she gives birth to a son on 20 May 1858. He is christened Maximiliano Leon José Manuel Enrique Bernardino, but will always be known just as Max. According to the local paper, at his christening 'there was present an immense assemblage who were attracted by the merry pealing of the bells, the cracking of sky rockets, and the gay tunes of a military band.'

The identity of the generous lover who was the father of

Max is hidden by Pepita from her mother but revealed in the book. According to this he is Lionel Sackville-West, an aristocratic young diplomat who had met her in Paris in the autumn of 1852. They had fallen deeply in love. They remained in love for nearly twenty years, until her death in 1871, and whenever Lionel could escape from his slow move up the diplomatic ladder in capitals all over Europe, he spent blissful days with her in villas in Germany and scattered over Italy, in homes in Heidelberg and Paris, and finally in a villa at Arcachon near Bordeaux, where he settled her for the last five or six years of her life.

But even though 'we know how sincerely they loved each other, and indeed the whole of their subsequent lives prove it', the relationship has its ups and downs, for ' Pepita was not an easy woman to hold, nor Lionel Sackville-West an easy-going lover.' Vita uses here what I think of as the Sitwell dot dot dot convention, because of Osbert Sitwell's inordinate fondness for it: '. . . It is idle to try to gloss over these things. She was a dancer, beautiful, desirable, and temptations were rife.' But in spite of such lapses, Lionel is her true love. The story ends with Pepita dying in childbirth with his name on her lips, and Lionel on his knees, sobbing by her corpse.

A resumé of the plot, compressing 140 pages into four, can give no idea of how enjoyable the book is to read. The understandable desire to romanticise one's ancestry has seldom been so attractively expressed. Unfortunately it is great nonsense – or at least enough of it is nonsense make one need to re-interpret the rest. One of these days someone may undertake the time-consuming task of going again through the lawyers' reports, and looking for other sources of information about Pepita and her career. But even on the basis of the evidence supplied in the book, one cannot help asking questions, and wondering why Vita Sackville-West's interpretation of events has been accepted for so long.

For one fact stands out from the story as told by Vita Sackville-West, even if she ignores it herself, and blows apart the romance in the fifteen-year relationship of Pepita and Lionel. Pepita's rich protector from at least 1855 to 1858, and the father of her first child Max, was clearly not Lionel Sackville-West at all. Catalina frequently boasted about his identity, and Pepita backed her up. From their talk, as recollected somewhat wildly by local people twenty or thirty years later, he was variously the Prince of Bavaria, the Prince of Metternich, the Emperor of Germany (there was no Emperor of Germany in the 1850s), or just 'a prince'. Similar stories were repeated in 1870 by the villagers at Arcachon, where Pepita now had a villa. The Prussian army was about to invade France, but Pepita, they said, on the basis of her own gossip, would be all right. Her eldest son was the son of the King of Bavaria, whose picture was hanging in her house.

His identity can be ascertained exactly. At Max's birth in 1858 he was declared in the register to be the son of his mother's legal husband Juan de la Oliva, with whom she had not been living for six years. This was respectable but clearly untrue. But his sponsor, as unexpectedly revealed in the register, was no less a personage than Duke Maximilian of Bavaria. According to Catalina, Max was named after his father. There can be little doubt that 'sponsor' was a euphemism concealing the truth of his paternity. Admittedly, Lionel later accepted Max as his son. Perhaps he even believed that he was; but in any case, as became clear in later years, he always did what Pepita wanted him to do.

Maximilian of Bavaria, known as the 'good duke' by the Bavarian people but regarded with less enthusiasm by his stuffier relatives, was a more colourful character than Lionel Sackville-West, and a much grander one. He was head of a junior branch of the Wittelsbachs, the Bavarian royal family. King Ludwig I, the lover of Lola Montez, and Ludwig II, the mad builder of castles and palaces, and patron of Wagner, were his cousins. He was related to most of the royal families of Europe, but loathed royal protocol, as did his doting daughter, Elizabeth, Empress of Austria, to the dismay of her Hapsburg in-laws. He preferred the company of writers, artists, circus people and peasants. He spent the summer roaming the forests round his castle of Possenhofen, in peasant dress, playing the zither at peasant weddings, but returning to his wife and castle to propagate another child. He was otherwise notoriously unfaithful, but his children adored him. He roamed Egypt and the Near East too, also playing the zither, and later writing a book about it. He was darkly handsome, a Byronic character perhaps, though those who did not like him might say pseudo-Byronic.

According to Vita Sackville-West, Pepita used talk to her mother about grand German lovers as a smokescreen to conceal her relationship with Lionel, her actual lover, whom she never mentioned to her. Some such explanation was needed to support her version of the story. But it is odd and unconvincing: what need was there for concealment? It is more likely that she did not mention him because of his unimportance: he was her little piece on the side, or one of several little pieces, and had the merit of being nineteen years younger than Maximilian.

Certainly Lionel was in no position to be a fount of gold and jewels. He was the fifth son of a moderately rich English earl, with no prospects, no way of knowing that he would ultimately inherit Knole, and only a modest income made up of the few hundred pounds a year normally the allocation of younger sons, plus the small salary of a diplomatic attaché.

His story in and after 1852 is curiously like that of Wilfrid Scawen Blunt, eleven years later. Blunt, like him, was in his early twenties, a diplomatic attaché with a private income of £400 a year. On holiday in Bordeaux, and very short of money, he was picked up in a fun fair by a pretty little woman dressed in black. She took him back to her lodgings and they made love. He was convinced that this was true love for ever. She took him to Biarritz, and paraded her beautiful and infatuated young admirer up and down the sands and promenade, where the court of Napoleon III were promenading too, and all its members seemed to know her. Blunt was in a state of intoxication about her, clothing her, as he later wrote, in 'a kind of supernatural innocence, impossible and absurd'. As his biographer Elizabeth Longford puts it, 'that he was penniless and living on her wealth, never troubled him'. But over the next few years he gradually realised where the wealth came from. These first weeks ended with his making a row about the attention paid to her by a Russian prince; she told him not to be a fool, and sent him back to his diplomatic life in Madrid. A year or so later, when he had been moved to Paris, her maid came unexpectedly to see him, said that her mistress was broke, wanted to meet up with him again, and would like him to find a little apartment for the two of them in Paris. Blunt could not resist the approach, and found three rooms in an attic for a rapturous reunion. But when she finally put in an appearance, she was living in a splendid apartment nearby in the Champs-Elysées; Blunt was left occupying his attic rooms on his own, but was allowed to visit her. One day, when doing so, he saw her in the window, in a clinch with an Irish lord, and that was that, for the time being.

Their third and last rapprochement was in London; she wrote that she was broke again, and for the first time asked him for money; he gave her a chunk of his little capital, and she welcomed him back. But when, on deciphering a letter printed on her blotting paper (that seems a bit sneaky of him), he found her writing in identical terms to a rich Jewish financier, he finally realised that true love was not her line, and broke off his affair with her for good. By then he had learned that she was not just Mrs or Miss Walters, as he had known her, but the notorious Skittles, the only English demi-mondaine to approach in style and success the great Parisian cocottes. When he first met her in 1868 she had just amicably finished her relationship with the Marquess of Hartington, collecting a settlement of £500 a year as a memento.

After his bitterness, which was considerable, had worn off, Blunt consoled himself by writing two sonnet sequences about their relationship; he moved on to numerous further affairs, and the two became good friends, and remained so until she died in 1920.

Unlike Scawen Blunt, Lionel Sackville-West did not give up; he was besotted with his delicious tart, and stuck it out for nineteen years. When he first met Pepita he believed, according to his own account, that she was a respectable dancer, only prevented from marrying him by her unhappy earlier marriage. He was young and innocent, and it was she who seduced him. The first of many disillusionments came soon after their first meeting; he heard that she was living in Munich with a Prince Yousoppof. This is related in *Pepita*, and also her miscarriage in 1868 by a relationship with an unknown lover. In between, or coterminously, came Duke Maximilian, and who knows who else; and it is hard to explain her sudden metamorphosis from failure in Madrid to success in Paris and Munich without positing an earlier unidentified sponsor and protector. Vita Sackville-West remarks of the villas in Germany, in Turin, in Como, in Genoa: 'Really those two must either have been very extravagant or very wealthy . . . for they proceeded to take Italian villas with a lavishness that is a little startling.' But, however financed, they were pursuing their happiness, as she put it, 'in almost idyllic circumstances in Italy, with their small Max growing up between them'. For Lionel it was perhaps less idyllic if he knew that it was 'her' not 'their' small Max who was growing up, and suspected that the villas were at least in part subsidised by richer lovers.

Lionel's nineteen-year relationship with Pepita seems to divide into two unequal portions. The period from 1852 to 1865 was a time for Pepita of professional success and many lovers, of whom Lionel was one. Then, in 1865, there was a change. She gave up dancing and settled down with Lionel into domestic life. Indeed, she tried to persuade him to contract a bigamous marriage with her. Then followed an odd episode: the British Consul at Malaga locked him in his room for three days to stop him going through with the marriage service. Lionel was the First Secretary in Madrid at the time, a good deal more important than the Consul: was the episode the result of collusion between them, to prevent the marriage without Lionel having to openly refuse to go through with it? But even without a marriage, Pepita induced him to act as though there had been one. They settled at Bordeaux, and then at Arcachon nearby, as husband and wife, and the four children whom she then had by him were all entered in the registers as the product of a legal marriage – one of Henry's strong cards in the law suit. Pepita enjoyed herself enlarging the villa, calling it the Villa Pepa and herself 'Comtesse West', and putting a coronet on her writing paper. This was not entirely ridiculous. The members of one nation are notoriously unable to understand the system of titles in others. 'The Honourable Mrs West' would have made little sense to French ears; Comtesse West was a reasonable equivalent. But the real countesses in the neighbourhood did not call on her. In the village 'the good-natured people said they were married, and the bad-natured people said they were not married'.

Why the change? Was it because her career as a dancer was on the decline and the supply of rich lovers was running out? Or, as Vita Sackville-West more charitably suggests, that 'after the effort and the excitement and the adulation, she was at last finding her natural fulfilment in domesticity and child rearing'. Certainly, Lionel Sackville-West, now an established senior diplomat, could give her security. At any rate, she appeared to settle down to a life of child-bearing, religion, good works and, according to the locals, the bottle; she put on weight and lost her looks.

In about 1868 there was another odd incident. Monsieur de Béon, the assistant stationmaster at Bordeaux, ushered into an empty railway carriage Lionel, Pepita, Duke Adalbert of Bavaria and his wife, the eldest daughter of the King of Spain. It is not clear whether the royal couple were on their way to Arcachon, or just passing through Bordeaux. Vita Sackville-West offers no explanation; in the light of her version of the story, no explanation is possible. But Adalbert was Duke Maximilian's nephew, and the most likely reason for the meeting is that he had come to see, or discuss the future of, little Maximiliano, now aged ten; Duke Maximilian may have been written to, to ask what he could do for his son. Whatever the explanation, the meeting was clearly amicable, for the Prince and Princess agreed to be sponsors of Pepita's forthcoming and fourth surviving child, christened Amalia Albertina; Henry, who caused all the trouble, was born in the following year.

The meeting had an unexpected sequel. The helpful stationmaster moved into the Villa Pepa as Pepita's secretary and agent. The locals had no doubt that he was also her lover, were appropriately scandalised, thought that the poor foreign count should chuck him out, but feared that he would not, because Pepita could make him do anything she liked. Vita Sackville-West finds it hard to accept stories of Pepita's drunkenness and of this last affair – 'Are we to believe that she deceived him, for whom she cared so tenderly?' – but has to admit that 'Pepita was unfathomable'. But was she unfathomable? Did she care so tenderly? Was she not predictably all of a piece – irresistible, at least in her early years, but always promiscuous; grateful, perhaps, to her devoted protector, but never in love with him?

After Pepita's death the problem arose of what to do with the five children, now aged from eleven to two. Lionel opted out. For a time Madame de Béon, the mother of his wife's reputed lover, moved into the villa and looked after them. During this time Lionel served as British Minister first in the Argentine, and then in Madrid. Meanwhile, Madame de Béon moved the children up to Paris, and Victoria was sent to a convent school, where she stayed, resentful and unhappy, for eight years. Then Madame de Béon died. By then Max had gone out to South Africa, where a farm had been bought for him. One may suspect that this was bought with Wittels-bach money, for Lionel, even if Max had been his son, was financially not in a good position to buy and stock farms in South Africa for others. Henry later went out to join Max. This left the three girls. A kindly English lady, whom Lionel had met in Buenos Aires and confided in, brought them over to her house in England. That was a welcome change for them; even better, although one of Lionel's two sisters, the Duchess of Bedford, ignored them, the other, the Countess of Derby, took them under her wing, and had them to her house in London (though when others came to call, the illegitimate brood were sent into another room).

In 1881 Lionel Sackville-West was appointed British Minister in Washington. Lady Derby lobbied Lord Granville, the Foreign Secretary; Lord Granville negotiated with President Arthur in Washington; and, amazingly, it was agreed that it would be acceptable for Sackville-West to bring his three illegitimate daughters to Washington, and for Victoria, the eldest, aged eighteen, to act as his ambassadress.

Washington fell for her. She received numerous proposals

of marriage in the seven years she was there, including one from the President, and turned them all down. She was voted 'the nicest girl in Washington'. She was as ravishing and full of vitality as her mother had been. To Lionel, she must have seemed a reincarnation of Pepita as she was when he first met her. One of Pepita's beauties was her hair which, when let down, fell gleamingly and abundantly to her knees; crowds used to gather in the street when she stood in the window combing it. Victoria's hair was equally long and lustrous. It was surely her father who had her photographed looking in a mirror and combing it – the photograph is reproduced in *Pepita*.

But was he her father? Vita Sackville-West knew that there was gossip about her mother's paternity, and dealt with it by putting up the wrong skittle and having no difficulty in knocking it down: 'I know full well that rumour has made the stationmaster into the true father of my mother, but chronologically that possibility is dispelled, since Pepita never met the stationmaster until after my mother was four or five years old.' But it is hard to see how one can categorically state that Lionel was her father, although this is now given as fact in biographies and guidebooks. In the baptismal register, when she was born in Paris in 1852, she is entered as the daughter of Josefa Duran (that is, of Pepita) and 'père inconnu'. There seem two main explanations for such 'père inconnu' entries: either the father wished to remain anonymous, or it was impossible to choose between two or more suspected fathers. Both are possible in Pepita's case. If the former, would Lionel, who was so ready to acknowledge paternity of her children from 1866 onwards, have refused to do so in 1862? It is not impossible, of course; but just as Duke Maximilian fathered Pepita's Maximiliano, it is tempting to look for a likely Victor to father Victoria (easy enough in Turin in the 1860s, but perhaps that is going too far).

Victoria told Vita that her mother 'thought it was a nice idea to call her daughter Victoria after the Queen of England'. This does not seem likely. Of course Victoria bore Lionel's surname and called him papa, but so did Max; as, years later, did P. G. Wodehouse's step-daughter Leonora, and step-children taken into other families.

And if Victoria had no blood relationship to Lionel, and Lionel knew it, what, if anything, could develop from that? Could it be . . . ? Here, there are major obstacles. The servants and Victoria's French companion would have had to be squared; Victoria never even hinted at it in later life. But it is perhaps just possible. And what a glorious sell it would have been if Lionel, who had managed so successfully to lead a double life as a diplomat, who had won official agreement to the installation of his illegitimate family in the embassy at Washington , had gone one step further – taken in the President and the whole of Washington society, and palmed his mistress off as his daughter?

10

P. G. Wodehouse: from hack to genius

A T SCHOOL at Ampleforth in Yorkshire I was taught
English for a time by Father Raphael Williams. He was a
dried-up old monk – or seemed old to me at the time – com-
monly known as 'Flaps'; he talked in a nasal voice like a
subdued version of the bleat of a goat, much imitated by us
schoolboys. But he was a good teacher; and when he told us,
in class one afternoon, that the two great masters of the
English language were Shakespeare and P. G. Wodehouse, I
took him seriously.

In fact Hilaire Belloc had said something similar, if less
sweeping, in what he wrote about Wodehouse in 1939, only a
few years before Father Raphael's dictum. I suspect that there
may have been a connection between the two opinions, or at
least a shared conversation. Father Raphael, like a number of
Ampleforth monks, used to take off in his short summer
holiday to tour from one country house to another and be
cosseted by high-born Catholic ladies. One of his ports of call
was Mells Manor in Somerset, the home of Raymond
Asquith's widow Katherine, and also frequented by Hilaire
Belloc, on a similar circuit. All that her granddaughter and
my friend Alice Jolliffe could remember of Belloc from her
childhood was how dirty he was, but I imagine that he and
Father Raphael, if their visits coincided, might have made
more contact.

It did not need much encouragement to turn me into a
Wodehouse fan. I read and re-read him all through my teens,

so much so that an Irish aunt (I was as well provided with aunts as Bertie Wooster) was much entertained, on seeing me helpless with laughter over one of his books and asking what it was that amused me, by being told that I was laughing at what I knew was coming on the next page.

I do not, unfortunately, have a full run of the original orange Wodehouses published by Herbert Jenkins, but the condition of the paperbacks on which I otherwise relied are evidence that my enthusiasm has continued till the present day. Through excessive use, they have broken up into fragments, chaotic to look at and often frustrating to read, since the odd page or pages have disappeared. This pathetic collection is not so large, however, for my taste in Wodehouse is selective. In his writing career of 75 years, from 1902 to 1977, he published 126 novels or books of short stories and 45 plays and musical comedies, quite apart from a vast amount of ephemeral journalism. It would not much worry me if all but 10 per cent or so of this, including all the plays and musical comedies, and all his books published before 1922 and after 1949, were to disappear. For the curious feature of Wodehouse's output appears to be that having poured out bilge for fifteen years or more the bilge suddenly turned to gold, then after twenty years reverted to bilge again for the last 28 years of his writing life. Moreover, even in the gold period he alternated gold with bilge, without appearing to notice the difference.

'Bilge' is an unkind word for work that is usually readable and sometimes entertaining. But the gold is not just the same only better; it is different in kind, and not just degree, from the bilge; it could almost have been written by a different person. And yet the elements are quite often the same: episodes, characters, metaphors and even sentences are re-used from earlier work, but in such a way that an explosion takes place and the bilge becomes gold.

Many writers have tried to analyse the secret of what is usually called 'vintage' Wodehouse, but which I would prefer to call 'gold', or perhaps 'alpha', because the alpha beta gamma system is clear and flexible. All his admirers must be grateful to Frances Donaldson in her *P. G. Wodehouse* (1982) for going carefully through the documentation of his years in Germany, and showing how ridiculous were accusations that he was a traitor, or even a collaborator, because of the broadcasts he made while in prison camp. But she embarked on the biography on the basis of her friendship with Wodehouse's stepdaughter, Leonora Cazalet, and at the suggestion of the Cazalet family, not because of any interest in or admiration of Wodehouse as a writer. She admits honestly that when she accepted the commission she was only an occasional and unenthusiastic reader of his books. She conscientiously sat down, however, and read through all 126 of them. She embodied the results in her opening chapter 'Introduction: The Master', which is remarkable for showing that she still had not the faintest idea of what he was about. Robert McCrane, in his biography of 2004, did not do any better.

Evelyn Waugh's 'Mr Wodehouse's idyllic world can never stale. He will continue to release future generations from a captivity which may be more irksome than our own, etc.' became wearisome from its repetition over the years on the back of the Penguin Wodehouses. It reads prettily, but little more; I prefer Hilaire Belloc, in his introduction to '*Week-End Wodehouse* (1939):

> The end of writing is the production in the reader's mind of a certain image and a certain emotion . . . the choosing of the right words and the putting of them in the right order. It is this which Mr Wodehouse does better in the English language than anyone else alive . . . he is unique for simplicity and exactitude, which is

as much as to say that he is unique for an avoidance of all frills. He gets the full effect, bang!

This is spot on for Wodehouse's style, but is not concerned with its content. Wodehouse himself made one of his rare perceptive remarks about this: 'I believe there are two ways of writing novels. One is mine, making a sort of musical comedy without music, and ignoring real life altogether; the other is going right deep down into life and not caring a damn.' This is excellent for Wodehouse as a whole, but what distinguishes alpha from beta and gamma Wodehouse is that it is musical comedy from which any hint of sentiment or sentimentality has been removed. No reader is going to feel a tug in the throat over Bingo Little's love affairs or be moved to pity by Bertie Wooster's predicaments. Sentiment is only introduced to be made fun of, as epitomised in the person of Madeline Basset.

Wodehouse had an extraordinary ear and eye for the absurd: for double meanings, ambiguities and clichés in English language and literature; for all the oddities and snobberies in English society; for other absurdities wherever he found or could create them. Armed with this equipment he moved into his chosen venue – London clubland, golf courses, country houses, village entertainments, briefly and gloriously Hollywood – and spun out of what he found there his own filigree structures, which only approximately relate to the basis of reality on which they are raised. 'Structure' is the wrong word, though, for work which is on the move, not static – moving with lightness, speed and economy to its conclusion, bang, bang, bang, and keeping the reader continuously delighted and amazed as it moves.

But trying to analyse Wodehouse makes one sympathise with the difficulties that others have experienced. Better, perhaps, to give the reader a short hors-d'oeuvres, the savour of which those who appreciate alpha Wodehouse will immediately recognise, though it may not mean much to those who do not.

I expected to find the fellow a wreck, but there he was, sitting up in bed, quite chirpy, reading *Gingery Stories*.

'What ho!' I said.

'What ho!' said Matty.

'What ho! What ho!'

'What ho! What ho! What ho!'

After that it seemed rather difficult to go on with the conversation.

Maiden Eggesford, like so many of our rural hamlets, is not at its best and brightest on a Sunday. When you have walked down the main street and looked at the Jubilee Watering-Trough, there is nothing much to do except go home and then come out again and walk down the main street once more and take another look at the Jubilee Watering-Trough.

'Mr Mulliner,' said Evangeline. 'Do sit down. Yes. I shall be glad to tell you anything you wish.'

Egbert sat down

'Are you fond of dogs, Miss Pembury?' he asked.

'I adore them,' said Evangeline.

'I should like, a little later, if I may,' said Egbert, 'to secure a snapshot of you being kind to a dog. Our readers appreciate these human touches, you understand?'

'Oh quite,' said Evangeline. 'I will send out for a dog.'

'Sir Jasper ffinch-ffarrowmere Bart,' he read. The name was strange to him.

'Show the gentleman in,' he said . . .

'Sir Jasper Finch-Farrowmere?' said Wilfred.

'ffinch-ffarrowmere,' corrected the visitor, his sensitive ear detecting the capital letters.

'Ah yes. You spell it with two small fs.'

'Four small fs.'

'This is a pretty state of affairs,' said the Mayor, breathing on the barrel of his revolver and polishing it on the sleeve of his coat. 'My daughter helping the foe of her family to fly – '

'Flee, Father,' corrected the girl, faintly.

'Flea or fly – this is no time for arguing about insects . . .'

'There is a man who really is a man. When he meets a gorilla, he laughs in its face.'

'Very rude.'

When I first got interested in looking for the beginnings of alpha Wodehouse I worked through my Penguins and Herbert Jenkinses and it seemed to me that its first appearance was in his book of golfing stories, *The Clicking of Cuthbert,* published in 1922. But I soon realised that the position was more complicated. Many of the novels, and even more the collections of short stories, first appeared, serialised in the case of the novels, in magazines, especially the *Saturday Evening Post* in America and the *Strand Magazine* in England, usually in both. Jeeves made his debut with Bertie Wooster in the story 'Extricating Young Gussie', first published in the *Saturday Evening Post* in the autumn of 1915, and printed in book form in *The Man with Two Left Feet*, published only in England, by Methuen in 1917. But the story is beta or even gamma Wodehouse, with a strong sentimental element. Jeeves is given two lines: 'Mrs Gregson to see you sir,' and 'Very good, sir. Which suit will you wear?' Bertie

Wooster has none of his later spark. For the general reader Jeeves and Bertie make their first proper and purely alpha appearance in *The Inimitable Jeeves,* published by Herbert Jenkins in 1923, shortly followed by *Carry On, Jeeves* in 1925. These are both collections of short stories, published earlier in magazines. Oddly enough, the earliest in origin of the stories are those in the second, 1925, volume, and the earliest of all of these, and the debut of alpha Jeeves and Bertie, is 'The Aunt and the Sluggard', first published in the *Saturday Evening Post* on 22 April 1916, followed by the *Strand Magazine* in August of the same year.

But there was an intermediate stage, between magazines and Herbert Jenkins, in the form of the book *My Man Jeeves,* published in 1919 by George Newnes, the firm which was also the publisher of the *Strand Magazine.* This contained the four original Jeeves and Bertie stories of 1916–17. The book did not sell well enough to go into a second edition; the four Jeeves stories were, with only minor changes, re-used by Herbert Jenkins in *Carry on Jeeves,* and *My Man Jeeves* was forgotten until republished in the invaluable new Everyman series in 2006.

The other four stories in *My Man Jeeves* were narrated by a character called Reggie Pepper, and dated originally from 1911 to 1915. Reggie Pepper, as has been recognised, was a pale prototype for Bertie Wooster; he was a young man of independent means, who tells the reader 'people have called me a silly ass' and that 'fellows, if you ask them, will tell you that I'm a chump. Well I don't mind. I admit it. I *am* a chump.' Three of the stories are very much beta Wodehouse, but the first, 'Helping Freddie', which was originally published in the *Strand Magazine* in September 1911, is the first sounding in Wodehouse's work of the alpha note both in story and language. Either Herbert Jenkins or Wodehouse himself must have realised that it was much the best of the

Reggie Pepper group and it was re-used in *Carry On Jeeves*, renamed 'Fixing it for Freddie' and remodelled as a Wooster–Jeeves story. Reggie Pepper became Bertie Wooster, Reggie's friend Jimmy Pinkerton became Jeeves, and a few necessary changes were made to feed them in, but otherwise it is word for word the original 1911 version. But it fits in with the other Wooster–Jeeves stories with no sense of difference.

In short, alpha Wodehouse first appears as early as September 1911 with 'Helping Freddie', and reappears five years later in the first four Wooster–Jeeves stories. After that Jeeves and Bertie pursue a triumphant progress through the 1920s and 1930s, and on into the 1940s, to be joined by the golfing stories in *The Clicking of Cuthbert* in 1922 (but some, at least, already published in magazines from 1911 on); by the Mr Mulliner stories, first collected with *Meet Mr Mulliner* in 1927; by the Drones stories, starting with *Young Men in Spats* in 1936; and by the five Hollywood stories, collected together in 1935, along with six Blandings Castle stories.

Nearly all these, with only occasional lapses, are pure alpha. But alpha Wodehouse was little valued when it first appeared, by Wodehouse or anyone else. There is no evidence that he thought it any better than his beta work, or that he or his publishers were conscious of his achieving a breakthrough when he wrote his first alpha stories before 1920. His reputation and his income derived from his collaboration with Guy Bolton and Jerome Kern on New York musicals, largely forgotten today, and four full-length novels published in increasingly well-paid instalments by the *Saturday Evening Post* between 1916 and 1919 and afterwards in book form in America and England: *Something Fresh*, *Uneasy Money*, *Piccadilly Jim* and *A Damsel in Distress*. These were all good beta stuff. The short stories were a sideline, which American publishers did not think worth collecting in a book (unlike, for instance, the short stories of Scott Fitzgerald), and their publication in England in 1919 was, as we have seen, not especially successful.

When Wodehouse embarked on a literary correspondence with his friend William Townend in 1920, his first letter included a resumé of his work to date. In this, he did not bother to mention Jeeves and Wooster. It was only when the letters were collected together in *Performing Flea* in 1953 that, with hindsight knowledge of their fame, a sentence was infiltrated into the published letter that was not in the original: 'I have managed to write a number of short stories for the SEP – about a bloke called Bertie Wooster and his valet.' For it was not until Herbert Jenkins published the couple in book form from 1923 onwards that they attracted a growing public, soon to be joined by the Oldest Member on the golf course, Mr Mulliner in the Angler's Rest, the young men of the Drones Club – along, of course, with Lord Emsworth and others at Blandings Castle, but this is a separate and somewhat peculiar story, of which more will be said later.

Between 1922 and 1949 Wodehouse wrote perhaps 16 alpha books. But the same period saw around 24 beta or even gamma ones. These are all, or nearly all, full-length novels, rather than collections of short stories. They often include a sentimental or moderately sentimental love story, and in many of them the hero is what Wodehouse called a 'buzzer' – a brash but decent young man on the make in the world, with a distinctive, flippant way of talking, and without the private income or subsidies from aunt or guardian which provides so much of the fun in alpha Wodehouse. Some continue to relate the adventures of characters who had appeared before 1920, most notably Psmith and Ukridge. Some feature comic policeman and burglars, who perhaps originated in the musical comedies. Many are based on a country house. One of the best, *Laughing Gas,* is placed in Hollywood. The collection vary much in quality: the best certainly have alpha elements but as a group they could be quietly eliminated without loss to Wodehouse's reputation.

If one goes to the letters in *Performing Flea* one gets little enlightenment from Wodehouse himself about his work. Alpha and beta books or stories both make an appearance, but are treated identically. The letters are almost exclusively involved with discussing plots – of both short stories and novels, but especially the latter. The assumption seems to be that if the plot is right the rest comes of itself. What value judgements there are suggest that Wodehouse was a bad critic of his own work. He describes, for instance, the plot of the short story 'Honeysuckle Cottage' as 'the funniest idea I have ever had', with which one might agree (though he says nothing about the pace, language and characterisation, which are at least as important as the plot), but calls 'The Coming of Gowf' 'the best golf story I have ever done', when in fact this feeble historical spoof is certainly the worst.

One gets the impression that he was essentially sales-led. If he found a line that sold well he would continue to produce it as long as it continued to do so, so that he ended up with several lines available, and had no feeling that one was any better than the other.

Lacking any help from Wodehouse himself, one has to make one own's guesses as to an explanation for alpha Wodehouse. At one stage I wondered if it had been set off by any event in his personal life, by inspiration derived from his meeting with Guy Bolton in 1915, by his marriage in 1914, or by his growing affection for his step-daughter Leonora, who became the person he loved best. But I could not produce any convincing reason for linking this development to any of them.

On the other hand, there is one technical explanation which makes sense, even if it does not provide a complete explanation. Wodehouse evolved his alpha style for his short stories. There is no doubt about this: between 1911 and 1929, it is only to be found in short stories. And in short stories Wodehouse, instead of having 300 plus or minus pages in which to make an impact, had to do it in 25 or so. Fast movement and what Belloc called 'the absence of all frills' was his technique to make them effective. Hence the wonderful compactness of the stories, and their reduction to the lightest and frothiest of elements, in which the love interest is conspicuously missing.

But, having evolved and exploited the technique through the 1920s, above all in the Bertie–Jeeves ones, in a happy moment Wodehouse tried applying the same technique to a full-length novel, and found that it could work. Hence Bertie and Jeeves in *Very Good Jeeves* (1930), *Thank You Jeeves* (1934), *Right Ho Jeeves* (1934), *The Code of the Woosters* (1938) and *The Mating Season* (1949). The trick was to devise these as a series of linked episodes, each episode related with the same brio as one of the short stories.

In curious contrast to the Jeeves–Wooster saga – short stories later developed into novels – is that of *Blandings Castle*, for this is one of novels developed into short stories.

Blandings Castle first featured in *Something Fresh*, serialised in the *Saturday Evening Post* (as *Something New*) in 1915, and published later on in the same year. Wodehouse was delighted by his breakthrough into the *Post*, but also amazed, for the subject was well outside its usual range. This was, however, one reason for its acceptance – the editor was intrigued by being taken into the strange world of English country-house life, upstairs and downstairs, and thought that his readers would be intrigued too.

So there first appeared not only Blandings Castle but a selection of its inhabitants – Lord Emsworth, the Honourable Freddy Threepwood, Beach the butler, the efficient Baxter, and an 'autocrat from Scotland' in the garden, not yet named

McAllister. But, however intriguing for American readers, *Something Fresh*, with its maundering jocularity, unconvincing love interest and sillyish plot, was an undistinguished book: only the character of Lord Emsworth gave hope for future developments. Its sequence *Leave it to Psmith* (1923) was not much better: it was the mixture as before, but with the addition of Psmith, who did not fit too well into the Blandings caste, and talked too much.

Then Wodehouse thought of trying out the same caste in short stories. Between 1924 and 1928 he wrote five of them, which were later published in 1935, along with one later Blandings story and five Hollywood ones, as *Blandings Castle*. With the application of his short-story technique, Blandings Castle sprung into life: two of the stories in particular – 'The Custody of the Pumpkin' and 'Pig-Hooey' (introducing the Empress of Blandings) – are, for most readers, the cynosure and epitome of the Blandings world.

A nice example of both the liberating effect on Wodehouse of shedding baggage and the creative way in which he re-used old material is to be found in two quotations, the first from the novel *Something Fresh* in 1915, the second from the short story 'The Custody of the Pumpkin', first published in the *Saturday Evening Post* in 1924. Both concern Lord Emsworth and Freddy Threepwood.

> Like many fathers in his rank of life, the Earl of Emsworth had suffered much through that problem which – with the exception of Mr Lloyd George – is practically the only fly in the British aristocratic amber – the problem of What to do with the Younger Son. It is useless to gloss over the fact, the Younger Son is not required. You might reason with a British peer by the hour – you might point out to him how, on the one hand, he is far better off than the male codfish, who

may at any moment find itself in the distressing position of being called on to provide for a family of over a million; and remind him, on the other, that every additional child he acquires means a corresponding rise for him in the estimation of ex-President Roosevelt; but you would not cheer him up in the least. He does not want the Younger Son.

In 1924 this shrunk to a quarter of the length and four times the effectiveness:

Unlike the male codfish, which, suddenly finding itself the parent of three million five hundred thousand little codfish, cheerfully resolves to love them all, the British aristocracy is apt to look with a somewhat jaundiced eye on its younger sons.

When Wodehouse went back to writing full-length Blandings stories, the resulting novels, starting with *Summer Lightning* in 1929, benefit from his short-story achievements and are far better than the earlier ones. Even so, they are also saddled with an inheritance from their predecessors. Glorious alpha passages are too often interspersed with tedious beta ones; above all, the love interest is unfortunately maintained, and one is faced, for instance, with gallant little Sue Brown ('a tiny thing, mostly large eyes and a wide, happy smile') and the supposedly tear-jerking episode when the equally gallant old trooper, Gally Threepwood, gives up the publication of his memoirs in order to enable her marriage to Ronald Fish ('she found herself crying, and was not ashamed').

Location seems to have made little difference to Wodehouse's writing. He produced a consistent output whether he was in New York, in London, in the English countryside or at Le Touquet, where the onset of war overtook him in 1939. He continued to produce in French and German prison-camps, in hotels in Berlin, and in apartments in Paris. Six novels were written in these years, and it is impossible to get any hint from them of his circumstances or to see any difference between them and their predecessors. One can only possibly wonder if the stresses he was under kept him, in the first five novels, to standard beta or at best beta-alpha productions; only in Paris in the spring and summer of 1946, with hopes of a return to England, did he feel joyful enough to go back to Jeeves and Bertie in *The Mating Season*, as good as anything he ever wrote.

But this is the swan-song of alpha Wodehouse. Because of the risk of prosecution as a collaborator, his return to England proved impossible, and early in 1947 he and his wife set off for America, where they were to live until his death in 1975. For two or three years he wrote effectively nothing, and lived off publishing the backlog of what he had written in the war years and in Paris, finishing with *The Mating Season*, published in 1949. But then he settled down to new work, and a steady stream of novels, stories and reminiscences came out at least once a year up till his death.

But the spark had gone. One can be romantic and wonder if the death of his step-daughter Leonora, which he first heard of in 1944, or what he saw as his rejection by England, broke something in him; but perhaps the failing creativity of old age is a more likely explanation. He could bring in the old characters or create new ones, and still devise likely plots for them, but the gaiety of alpha language and dialogue eluded him.

And so for twenty years and more the amiable husk and hermit of Rensenburg, New York, did the crossword, exercised his dogs and tapped away at his typewriter, until knighthood and acceptance by England came to him in 1975, six weeks before his death and too late to be of any use.

11
How to write a bestseller:
Evelyn Waugh and Nancy Mitford

WHEN I WAS ON HOLIDAY in Ireland in 1946, my uncle came back from shopping in Waterford with *Brideshead Revisited*. He was not a great reader; I don't know why he bought it. His books, such as they were, were kept in the little room, rather charmingly known as the book room, in which we normally sat in preference to the drawing room, with its high Georgian windows and long views. The book room was poky. We sat in it in the long summer twilight, while my aunt knitted by the flickering light of a table lamp, powered, not very efficiently, by a generator across the lawn. Whenever she paused to talk and stopped knitting, she would turn the light off, for economy. My uncle, though the sweetest of men, was careful about money.

He found *Brideshead* 'disgusting', but it was left lying around, and I, aged 14 or so, took it to an upstairs lavatory to read. I remember this little room well, though uncle, aunt, and house have long since passed on, or out of my life. It was at the end of the main bedroom corridor, with a glass panel over the door, to light the corridor. Once I started reading I could not stop, and only with difficulty could get off the lavatory seat two or three hours later.

All over England, for the next ten years or so, and at intervals in succeeding decades, people of all ages were also paying the book tribute in their own ways: babies by the dozen emerged from the font as Sebastians, and too often never recovered from it; embarrassing flocks of teddy bears descended on the universities.

I am not alone in now finding *Brideshead* rather awful, if still intensely readable. Waugh himself, who thought he had written a masterpiece, was disconcerted by the reactions of what he called the 'highbrows', friendly or otherwise: 'it lost me such esteem as I once enjoyed among my contemporaries,' he wrote in the preface to the 1960 edition, in which he claimed to have pruned the text of its worst excesses. One of the most slashing reviews was by Edmund Wilson, the New York critic. Waugh, who professed to despise all things American and had told his agent, 'I should not think six Americans will understand it,' could write Wilson off as 'an insignificant Yank'; what he found unbearable was the book's success with the ghastly American public. They lapped it up, lords and all.

In March 1944, in the early heady days of composition, he told his friend Coot Lygon, 'I am writing a very beautiful book, to bring tears, about very rich, beautiful, high-born people who live in palaces and have no troubles except what they make themselves and these are mainly the demons sex and drink, which after all are easy to bear as troubles go nowadays.' But in May he wrote to his agent that the book was 'steeped in theology'; in January he told Nancy Mitford that 'the book is about God'; in his 1960 preface he described its theme as 'the operation of divine grace on a group of diverse but closely connected characters'. He could have been writing about two different books, but was not.

The religious theme (one can wonder if it was there from the start) was what he hoped was going to lift him in critical estimation from a comic to a serious novelist; when he referred to *Brideshead* as 'the magnum opus' or 'mag. op.', or took over Nancy Mitford's description of it as the GEC (Great English Classic), he was more than half-serious. But the description, so very different in tone and content, sent to Coot Lygon cannot just be written off as making fun of himself and his work in the way he always wrote to her. His letter chimes in with one of the reasons that he listed when he wrote to the War Office, asking for leave in which to write a novel: that writing it would get rid of 'the financial uncertainty caused by the necessity of supporting a large family [three, and a fourth on the way] on the pay of a lieutenant'. He wanted to write a masterpiece; but he also wanted to write a bestseller and make a lot of money.

Christopher Sykes, in the ponderous and unilluminating 'discussions' of each novel which interrupt his pioneer biography of Evelyn Waugh, suggests Thackeray's *Henry Esmond* as a possible model for *Brideshead*. I cannot see the slightest resemblance. If one was to look for a model I would offer, half-seriously, Daphne du Maurier's *Rebecca*, the great bestseller of the immediate pre-war years, the 29th impression of which came out a few months before Waugh wrote to the War Office. *Rebecca* presents a hero nobly named Max de Winter; a great house, which is a character in the novel as much as a setting for it; a sadder and wiser narrator who returns to it – 'Last night I dreamt I went to Manderley again'; and dollops of the lush, over-charged but fast-moving language which could be described as best-sellerese. Waugh provided a nobler caste, a grander house, and even lusher language. One may or may not be moved by his religious theme. But it was not this that hoisted it into the bestseller lists and took it, night after night, on to the television screen or, for that matter, glued me to my lavatory seat: it was the lovely luscious wallow in high life, sex and scandal; the dome, frescoes and fountains; the gilded youth disporting in Oxford cloisters; the beautiful young lord taking to the bottle; the hero making free of the narrow loins of a marquess's daughter in an Atlantic gale; the marquess dying in his huge four-poster bed in the chinoiserie drawing-room of a Palladian palace. To which should perhaps be added the whimsical teddy bear.

By 1944, Waugh had penetrated far enough into country-house life and country-house families; he had indeed twice married into them. He could produce something more socially convincing than Lord Peter Wimsey. But he had not risen as far as 'very rich, high-born people who live in palaces', the ten or twenty families with a great house in the country, a great house in London, great wealth, and eligibility for marriage with royalty. So he had to cobble his Flytes together, out of gossip, imagination, reading and the customary trick of all writers of what at one time were called silver-fork novels: to take people and situations one knew, and promote them several steps up the social ladder.

It might seem odd that he made so little use of the family which came closest to what he was looking for, and which would, it might seem, have needed only a little aggrandisement to fill the bill – the Lygons of Madresfield. They did, in fact, provide the fictional structure: the father in exile, the mother and children living on in the big house, the younger son who drank too much and died young. But, as Waugh explained to Coot Lygon, his most beloved of the daughters: 'It's all about a family whose father lives abroad, as it were Boom [Lord Beauchamp] – but it's not Boom – and a younger son: people will say he's like Hughie, but you'll see he's not really Hughie – and there's a house as it might be Mad, but it isn't really Mad.'

The descendants of the Lygons are understandably eager to promote the image of Madresfield by identifying it with Brideshead, and the Lygons with the Flytes. But there is no reason to suppose that Waugh was not being straightforward with Coot; his book bears him out. The Lygons brought out all that was most attractive in him; the times he spent there as a young man (all post-Oxford) were ones of happiness and laughter without emotional involvements; Coot and her sister Mamie remained his dear friends. But they did not provide what he was looking for for Brideshead. Madresfield itself was by origin a modest moated manor house, which had been much inflated in Victorian times; there are elements of it in Hetton Grange in *A Handful of Dust*, written, in fact, in Waugh's Madresfield period, before the house was shut out to him and the sisters by their brother's marriage to a (by them) much-hated Danish wife in 1936. Apart from the Art Nouveau chapel, Brideshead owes nothing to Madresfield. Its dome, fountain and eighteenth-century grandeur came from Castle Howard, which Waugh had gone over to see when at Ampleforth (I think on a retreat) in 1937; no doubt other Baroque or Palladian mansions contributed, whether known at first hand or culled from *Country Life* and Tipping's *In English Homes*.

There were no young lords being whimsical with teddy bears in grand English houses around 1930. There were no young Lord Sebastians either. As Oscar Wilde's biographer puts it, St Sebastian, young, naked and liberally stuck with arrows, 'always iconographically attractive, is the favourite saint amongst homosexuals'. Wilde assumed the alias Sebastian Melmoth when he came out of prison; Andre Raffalovich, the outrageously camp friend and benefactor of Aubrey Beardsley, was finally admitted to the Third Order of Dominicans as Brother Sebastian. But, perhaps not surprisingly, Sebastian was not an upper-class English name.

It is accepted that the principal model for Sebastian was Waugh's friend Alistair Graham; indeed, on occasions in the original manuscript he absent-mindedly wrote 'Alistair' instead of 'Sebastian'. He may have given Sebastian Hugh Lygon's good looks, charm and title, upped from Honourable to Lord; but it is the recollection and fictional transformation of his Oxford and immediately post-Oxford affair with Graham which gives *Brideshead* its main emotional charge.

Graham had what used to be called 'good connections', but was no aristocrat. His rich, bossy American mother had already been promoted by Waugh to serve as Lady Circumference in *Decline and Fall*. If Charles Ryder's escape from Oxford to an empty Brideshead is based on anything, it is probably on an escape to Barford House, the Grahams' handsome but moderate-sized country house outside Warwick, when free of Mrs Graham.

Graham remains a mysterious character; he and Waugh drifted apart in the 1930s, and he ended his life as a recluse (an alcoholic one?) in Wales. But what was he like? How closely did he resemble Sebastian? I was amused to come across a description of him when attached to the British Embassy in Athens, written by Georgia Sitwell in 1929: 'an utterly spineless very affected lady-like young man . . . not at all amusing and full of airs'. But since on the one occasion I stayed with Georgia and Sacheverell Sitwell in the 1960s I took an immediate and violent dislike to her, I would not rely on her judgement.

Alistair Graham may or may not have had a teddy bear; John Betjeman certainly did, and Waugh knew him well. The similarities between Sebastian's Aloysius and Betjeman's Archie and the way in which the two men paraded, talked or wrote about their bears, seem too close to be coincidence, and so the 'middle-class little Dutchman with dirty teeth', as those who failed to appreciate Betjeman's quality wrote him off, made his contribution to Sebastian. But Waugh was, on and off, a genius, and out of diverse and by no means all aristocratic elements he created a memorable character. Nature imitates art; the owner's teddy bear features prominently in at least one country-house guidebook today.

Agreeable games can be and have been played with the other characters. Anthony Blanche is convincingly recognised as an amalgam of Harold Acton and Brian Howard. Mr Samgrass is less convincingly said to be based either on Maurice Bowra or 'Sligger' Urquhart (he is awfully like Jack, later Sir John Plumb, but dates and locations do not seem to fit). Rex Mottram is apparently close to Brendan Bracken. For the Marchmains, other than Sebastian, nothing convincing has been put forward. I can make a small contribution. Lady Marchmain is engaged in putting together a book in memory of her two brothers, killed in the war. The results sound close to the book of memories, photographs and extracts from letters put together by Lady Desborough in memory of her dead sons Julian and Billy Grenfell. Lady Marchmain's rugged brothers are reminiscent of photographs of Julian. The book was privately printed, but was certainly on the shelves or occasional tables of the Herberts' Pixton, the Asquiths' Mells, and other houses frequented by Waugh. I don't know that he ever met Lady Desborough; but he may have seen through the pious text to the killer-mother, later to be analysed with brilliance by Nicholas Mosley.

For the 1960 edition, Waugh analysed the style in which the book was written, for many a chief stumbling block to its appreciation. *Brideshead* was the product of 'a bleak period of present privation and threatening disaster . . . and in consequence the book is infused with a kind of gluttony, for food and wine, for the splendours of the recent past, and for rhetorical and ornamental language, which now written with a full stomach I find distasteful.' To this might be added the pent-up frustration of his failure to be accepted as an officer and a gentleman, and nostalgia for his Oxford life and loves. Anyway, once he had installed himself in a country-house hotel in Devon, the hatches burst and it all came spilling out, the spirit of Ethel M. Dell with frisking round her all the metaphors for which he had increasingly had a weakness but had kept under control.

When powered by the strong feeling of his Oxford life and loves he can carry the reader along. But once Sebastian has sunk beneath his sea of alcohol the impetus is lost. Julia barely exists; Lord Marchmain is an off-the-shelf elderly aristocrat; Cordelia a stock convent girl; the nanny a stock nanny. Emotionally the book was subsiding, and had to be inflated with literary wind, which Waugh, now in full tilt, took for inspiration; hence the two appalling monologues, of Julia by the fountain and Lord Marchmain on his deathbed.

Lord Marchmain's death is another example of promotion. A final repentance and making the sign of the cross had been witnessed by Waugh at the deathbed of his old friend Hubert Duggan in 1943, and had deeply moved him. But it took place in the bedroom of a small house in South Street, Mayfair. Its elevation to the chinoiserie drawing-room at Brideshead is upsetting; there is a vulgarity about using it in this way.

In its later stages the book is rescued by the brilliance of its minor characters, newly introduced or continued from the first half: by the odious Mr Samgrass, the ghastly Lady Celia, Charles Ryder's slyly malicious father, the absurd Mrs Muspratt (and 'Bridey' too), the brash Rex Mottram, and perhaps above all Anthony Blanche. But is Blanche a minor character? From one angle he is the hero of the book, a character who remains true to his principles. In Oxford days he warned Charles Ryder against the insidious dangers of upper-class charm and of the desire to be English gentlemen which has destroyed too many English artists. Later on he goes to Ryder's exhibition in London and, in a gay bar nearby, wryly points out that charm has won: 'It kills love; it kills art; I greatly fear, my dear Charles, it has killed *you*.' But Charles Ryder does not respond to the twitch of this particular thread.

The Pursuit of Love and *Love in a Cold Climate* inevitably get linked with *Brideshead Revisited*. The three novels appeared within a few years of each other. All three were best-sellers, everyday stories of upper-class life inexorably destined for film and television. The two writers were friends; Waugh suggested the title for *The Pursuit of Love*, gave Nancy Mitford advice and criticism for both books, and rejoiced in her success.

But whereas Waugh, after his masterpieces of previous decades, produced a novel which embarrassed his admirers, Nancy Mitford, after four slight and mildly amusing novels published between 1931 and 1940, and a gap of five years, wrote two deservedly enduring classics. The contrast was perhaps partly due to her earlier novels being inspired by her circle of silly if entertaining friends – Hamish Erskine, Mark Ogilvie-Grant and others – whereas for their two successors she went back to her own childhood and early years. The vividness which accrues to all reminiscences of childhood was spiced up by the eccentricity and originality of her family.

The Pursuit of Love was a novel, not autobiography. Very reasonably, she adjusted the autobiographical elements to fit the story. But it is amusing to see how the book has been taken as straight autobiography, so that the blurb to its Penguin editions can write of 'her childhood in a large remote country house'. The Radletts of *The Pursuit of Love* did indeed live, and had lived for generations as a succession of 'bucolic squires', in a 'large, ugly, north-facing Georgian house . . . as grim and bare as a barracks, stuck up on the high hillside', full of 'heads of beasts, with the flags and uniforms of bygone Radletts'. The Mitford story was different; and the differences were more likely to have produced a family like the Radletts than the background given to them in the novel.

The Mitfords of Mitford in Northumberland were ancient northern gentry, but the Redesdale Mitfords belonged to a

younger branch that had gone south and produced merchants, bankers, lawyers, diplomats, writers and civil servants rather than soldiers or bucolic squires. A younger son in
the early ninetheenth century was a successful lawyer and
Lord Chancellor of Ireland; he was created Baron (and his
son, later, Earl of) Redesdale, and from a distant Freeman
cousin inherited Batsford Park in Gloucestershire, and eleven
thousand acres in Gloucestershire, Oxfordshire and War-
wickshire.

Nancy Mitford's grandfather was well known in his day, a
late Victorian swell, man-about-town and friend of the Prince
of Wales, who after an adventurous youth as traveller and
diplomat in Russia, China and Japan spent twelve years as
Secretary to the Board of Works (in charge, amongst other
things, of the royal palaces). Apart from a house in London
and a villa at Westgate-on-Sea, he was landless; but in 1886
when he was aged 49 his distant cousin the Earl of Redesdale
died, and unexpectedly left him all his property. So he gave up
his Civil Service job and had a lovely time.

He rebuilt the agreeably Georgian Batsford Park as a neo-
Elizabethan mansion double its size, complete with ballroom
and great hall. He made what became a famous garden
around it, thick with bamboo groves and Japanese sculpture.
He built a stud farm in which to breed Suffolk Punches. He
presented the neighbouring town of Moreton-in-the-Marsh
with a large Redesdale Hall, commanding the town from an
island site in the main street. As a local worthy, he served as
MP for Stratford-upon-Avon in 1892–95, and in 1902 the
title of Lord Redesdale was recreated for him. But well before
his death in 1916 it became clear that Batsford Park and its
adjoining estates would have to be sold to pay his debts.

Nancy Mitford's father was his second son. He was a
brave volunteer in both the Boer and the 1914–18 wars but
was never a regular soldier and, between the wars, as a

younger son without money, worked not too happily on the staff of *The Lady*, which his father-in-law owned. Nancy Mitford was brought up until she was eleven in a house in London and converted cottages by a mill near High Wycombe. Then, in 1915, her father's elder brother was killed. As he left a pregnant widow, the future of the five (later seven) little Mitfords as Hons remained in doubt until their aunt gave birth to a daughter five months later. Their father was now heir to title, land, and debts. By the time the debts were paid off, the new Lord Redesdale was left with a moderate estate and income and numerous children. Money was tight, and his efforts to increase his income by, amongst other ploys, digging for gold in Canada, were notably unsuccessful. The short fuse on which he lived, so vividly portrayed in the novels, was perhaps the result.

On the death of his brother, he and his family had moved into a house in the village at Batsford, and briefly into Batsford Park itself when the first Lord Redesdale died. But the house was on the market, and they did little more than camp out in it. Once it was sold the family estates consisted of two thousand acres in Oxfordshire, a good deal of moorland in Northumberland, and no proper house. In 1917 Lord Redesdale accordingly bought Asthall Manor on the southern fringe of his Oxfordshire property – not a Georgian house on a hill, but a Jacobean manor lying snugly in a valley, on the edge of the village and next to the church. It was not until 1927, or thereabouts, that he completed a new house in the centre of his estate a mile or two north of Swinbrook. Of the numerous houses in which the Mitford children were brought up, this was the only one that bore any relationship to the Radletts' Alconleigh; it was indeed a remote, ugly, Georgian house on a hillside – but a neo-Georgian one.

The children had been happy in Asthall, and all of them except Debo, the youngest, much disliked the new house.

Nancy was in her early twenties when it was built, but lack of funds compelled her to spend more time there than she liked until she married in 1933.

It is a good story, but a complicated one, and not what Nancy Mitford wanted. She was after something much simpler – a nice clean contrast between the Radletts, who loved the land on which they had lived for generations, and the new-rich Kroesigs, who loved their money. Surprise is sometimes expressed that Lord Redesdale enjoyed his representation as the fearsome Uncle Matthew; but perhaps he liked it because it gave him the history and background that he would have liked to have.

Nancy Mitford wrote *The Pursuit of Love* independently of *Brideshead Revisited*, not as a story about 'very grand people who live in palaces', but as a distillation from her own less grand family. But she wrote *Love in a Cold Climate* after *Brideshead* had come out, and been a bestseller, and jumped on the *Brideshead* bandwagon, as she honestly states in the first three lines of the book: 'It is necessary to emphasise the fact once and for all that the Hamptons were very grand as well as very rich.' But she did not copy. Her grand house was as different as possible from Brideshead, and her grand family bore no resemblance to the Flytes. Both she and Waugh had a merry time disporting in their chosen field of high life. But Waugh could stifle any doubts that what he was doing was not quite respectable by injecting his story with religion. Nancy Mitford had no hang-ups, and not much religion; she just enjoyed herself.

As she had only penetrated to the fringes of such a grand world (visits to her sister at Chatsworth were in the future), she had to extemporise just as much as Evelyn Waugh. Her husband's aunt, Mrs Stuart-Wortley, lived at Highcliffe Castle in Hampshire, built by Lord Stuart de Redcliffe in 1830–34 and somewhat crazily incorporating re-erected portions of a fifteenth-century French chateau. The result was a palatial seaside villa on a small estate rather than a great country house, but suitably inflated and set in a landscape of radiating avenues it became the Hamptons' Hampton Park. As owner of the house, she created Lord Montdore, unmistakeably derived in part from the Fifth Marquess of Lansdowne. Lansdowne, like Montdore, had been Viceroy of India, had a taste for the classics, and in 1917 had written a famous and controversial letter advocating that the war should be ended by negotiation. His biographer describes him as 'the very finest type of what the old patrician system of this country could produce', and quotes a political opponent calling him 'the very best type of British aristocrat'. Lord Montdore was 'the very type of English nobleman . . . even Socialists conceding his excellence, which they could afford to do, as there was only one of him and he was getting on.' There seems a strong streak of personal malice in her portrait, and yet it is unlikely that she ever met Lord Lansdowne; perhaps she heard of him from his granddaughter Margaret Mercer-Nairne, who was for a time her sister Diana's best friend, or her father had had dealings with him in the House of Lords, and she had had an overdose of his praises; or perhaps, flipping through his biography and its illustrations, or seeing the photographs of himself which he sent out as a Christmas card to at least one of his grandchildren (my mother) in 1922, and surveying the stiff, beautifully turned out old patrician with his white wing collar echoing his white moustaches, she might have been inspired to write of Lord Montdore as 'wonderful old cardboard', who seemed 'a wonderful old fraud', to 'two irreverent little girls'.

Neither Lady Montdore nor Polly, nor Polly's story, have any prototypes in the Lansdowne family. For elements of Lady Montdore and for Polly, the beloved only child, and her marriage to her uncle 'the lecherous lecturer', Nancy Mitford may have drawn on another grand family, whose history she is most likely to have known.

The 10th Earl of Scarbrough, owner of Lumley Castle and Sandbeck Park, and his wife, who came from a rich but much less grand background, had an only child, a daughter. The bulk of his estates, including the two great houses, was entailed on his nephew, but even so his daughter Serena was an heiress. In 1923, aged 22, she married Bobby James, a younger son of Lord Northbourne, who was old enough to be her father, and had been married before (the year before she was born) to a sister of the Duke of Wellington. My father, who was a friend of Serena for fifty years or more, used to tell me a story which I think was basically true (if improved in the telling) that Bobby James's son Arthur had proposed to Serena, who told him that she was very sorry, but she had just agreed to marry his father.

Lady Scarbrough was famous for her malapropisms, and used to talk about 'flying buttocks' instead of 'flying buttresses', just as Lady Montdore talked about 'suppository' for 'repository' and 'daisy' for 'pansy'. Bobby James (whose family's property in Northumberland bordered that of the Mitfords) was not Serena's uncle, but – in a way too convoluted to be worth explaining – he was the uncle by marriage of her half-sister. This was Dorothy Wellesley, poetess and drunk, whose husband Lord Gerald Wellesley later became the 7th Duke of Wellington. Someone (but who? I think not my father, possibly the Duke of Wellington) upset me considerably by assuring me that Bobby James was the model for the Lecherous Lecturer. I was upset because when, as a shyish teenager, I went to stay with him and Serena not long before he died he had been extremely nice to me. Polly herself bears no relationship to Serena James.

Surmising origins for characters is perhaps more entertaining than useful. What is impressive is the élan of the two stories, and the skill with which they are put together. Admittedly, *The Pursuit of Love* depends more on the vividness of the portraits of the Radletts than the story line; but in *Love in a Cold Climate*, in which the Radletts have retired into the background, the relationship between the four main characters – Lady Hampton, Polly, 'Boy' and Cedric – is beautifully worked out. The snob element is enjoyable enough, but there is more to the books than snobbery. However, I fear it is snob appeal to which they owe their continuing success. It is rather depressing to look at the 1980 Penguin joint edition of the two books. Groups of Radletts and Hamptons dolled up for a ball in ersatz aristocratic splendour, as in the 'glittering Thames Television serial', entice the potential reader to buy 'these delicious, utterly wicked, and compulsively delightful exposés of the English upper crust . . . from the pen of one who knows.' Such are the penalties for writing a bestseller.

12

Waugh on Girouard: a correction

'MONDAY 25 June 1955. Thomas Pakenham came for the night at his invitation, brought by Dick Girouard's son, Mark. He is a handsome lad marred by spots, awkward in manner, painfully self-assertive. Girouard out-shone him, recognising Burges's wash-handstand as soon as he saw it, and exhibiting remarkable knowledge of English nineteenth-century art. Both boys refused champagne saying they were surfeited with it.'

It was I who was the spotty boy. Thomas Pakenham has never ceased to resent this transference of my spots to him.

13

The Solomons

ABOUT HALF-WAY along St Dunstan's Street, the long street that leads north-west out of Canterbury, the row of houses is broken by a small alleyway, scarcely large enough to be called a yard, and closed off after fifty feet or so by a wall and a locked door. Like all such cul-de-sacs it tends to be used as a dump, and a pile of rubbish blocks the wall but also acts as a useful ascent by which one can look over it. When I climbed this I knew, in theory, what I would see on the other side, but what I actually saw filled me with an unexpected surge of delight. Hidden by the wall was a space a little larger than a tennis court, enclosed on all sides, carpeted like a meadow with long grass and buttercups, and quiet and peaceful in the evening sun. Out of the grass projected a hundred or more gravestones, mostly of the late eighteenth and early nineteenth centuries, none at all elaborate, and all, in strange contrast with their rustic English setting, inscribed with Hebrew lettering.

No one could have failed to be intrigued by this quiet oasis of the dead, but for me it had an especial significance. One of the gravestones commemorated Nathaniel or Nathan Solomon of Margate, who died in 1793 and had attended the synagogue in Canterbury, long since closed. He was of interest to me partly for himself but even more for his descendants, of whom, by way of St Helena, Cape Town and Pretoria, I am one.

Nathan is my first traceable Solomon ancestor. He was in business as a jeweller and clock-maker at Margate in Kent by 1766–7, when he was admitted as a member of the Great Synagogue in London. I don't know if this means that he had started life in London; it would make sense if he had gone from there to exploit business opportunities in Margate, which was just coming into fashion as a seaside resort, and was a flourishing small port as well.

He married, probably in the 1760s, a wife of Dutch origin, Phoebe de Metz or Mitz, and died in 1793. It used to be said that Phoebe was the sister of the Matilda de Metz who married a London merchant, Levy Salomons, and was the mother of Sir David Salomons, Bart., the first Jewish Lord Mayor of London and the second Jewish MP. The dates don't fit, though Phoebe may have been Matilda's aunt. In any case, I suspect that it was the de Metz rather than the Solomon blood which set off the remarkable flowering of their descendants. According to a story retailed in Louis Herrman's *A History of the Jews in South Africa* and elsewhere, she lived to 104, and had 21 children. In fact, she died aged 92, and my father could only trace nine children, though there may well have been more. Her portrait in old age (said, unconvincingly, in the family to be by Opie) suggests that she had a strong character. When the portrait was hanging in the Solomon house in Cape Town its beady eyes seemed to follow her little great-grandchildren wherever they were in the room, and they were in awe of it.

There was no synagogue at Margate; the Solomons attended the one at Canterbury, which had been in existence since 1760, and possibly earlier. Around 1800 various Solomons, mostly trading either as jewellers or naval provisioners, also appear elsewhere round the Kent coast, at Chatham, Deal, Sheerness and Ramsgate. Some may have been Nathan's sons, as may Henry Solomon, Chief Constable of Brighton, who was murdered by a prisoner in 1844.

Four of his sons migrated to St Helena. The first to settle there was Saul, born probably in 1776, and in St Helena by about 1796. According to family legend he was on a ship bound for India, became sick, and was carried ashore at St Helena to die. True or not, he became a soldier in the St Helena Regiment, which was run, like the island, by the East India Company, and was a sergeant in it by 1802, when he set up a canteen in the barracks. By 1810 he had left the army, and was living in Jamestown, St Helena's one town, and as founder and proprietor of the St Helena Press was doing all the printing on the island, official and unofficial. After that he grew steadily more prosperous until, as printer, hotelier, store owner, property owner, trader and planter, he was the most important person on the island, outside the government and military establishment, and was known (I am never quite sure by whom, other than by his descendants) as 'the Merchant King of St Helena'. From the late 1790s onward four of his brothers – Charles, Benjamin, my direct ancestor Joseph, and Lewis Gideon – followed him to St Helena, as did Isaac Moss, whose sister Hannah married Joseph. Originally he traded as Solomon, Dickson and Taylor; later Lewis Gideon, who had taken Gideon instead of Solomon as his surname, and Isaac Moss joined with him to form what became the well-known firm of Solomon, Moss, Gideon and Company.

In those days St Helena was not a remote and forgotten island. It was the place where ships bound for South Africa and round the Cape to India stopped to break the journey and take in supplies. A great boost for the prosperity of the island, and of the Solomons with it, came with the arrival of Napoleon in 1815, along with a large entourage and household and several thousand extra soldiers to guard him. Saul's brother Lewis Gideon had followed one strand of the family tradition and set up as a jeweller, horologist and silversmith. He looked after the government clocks and, in addition, became the 'Imperial Horologist' and went regularly up to Longwood to wind the clocks. In his first year on St Helena, Napoleon, as part of his running battle with the Governor Sir Hudson Lowe, complained that his allowance was insufficient, and to raise money and make a gesture had his insignia hammered off his silver (or some of it) and sold it to Lewis Gideon. This is a well-attested incident, unlike another family story about the Solomons in those days. Saul and his brothers had plotted to enable Napoleon to escape, a ship was waiting at the foot of the cliff, and a silk ladder smuggled into Longwood in a teapot. The ladder was discovered, and the plot foiled. This story is almost certainly apocryphal, but it is true that Hudson Lowe included the Solomons in a list of Napoleonic sympathisers. With Lewis Gideon winding the clocks at Longwood, and Saul trading overseas from Jamestown, they were well positioned to smuggle letters in and out of Longwood and St Helena; officially, all Napoleon's correspondence had to be vetted by the Governor.

When Napoleon died in 1821, the Solomons were among those who filed past at his lying in state and attended his funeral. Joseph's eldest son Henry, then aged five, vividly remembered how 'he had looked with awe into the grave; how very deep it seemed to him, and how the soldiers stood around when the body of the exiled Emperor was laid to rest, how bitterly the French soldiers wept, and his own mother, who held his hand, wept also. She had taken him, before the body left Longwood, to see the Emperor lying in state, she had lifted him up to see the quiet face, and had stooped to kiss the dead hand.'

In 1840 the Prince de Joinville arrived in a French ship at St Helena to disinter Napoleon's body and convey it to the

Invalides in Paris. Saul Solomon was one of the leading people involved in receiving the Prince and helping with arrangements for the disinterment. By then he was serving as French and Dutch consul, and Sheriff of St Helena. Amongst the properties owned by him all over the island was the house known as The Briars, with its adjacent pavilion, in which Napoleon had lived while Longwood was being got ready for him; Saul is said to have preserved it in the same state and with the same internal arrangement as used by the Emperor. It was probably in these later days of affluence and respectability that an incident related by Saul's nephew Henry occurred. The Governor sent to ask him for the loan of his silver plate, for use at a dinner which he was giving to a distinguished visitor to the island. 'Saul Solomon replied that as he was to entertain the same guest to dinner on the following evening, and as it might be thought that he himself had borrowed his Excellency's plate for the occasion, he begged to be excused from complying with the request.'

Saul Solomon married three times and died in 1852 at Portishead on the Bristol Channel, the home of his son-in-law, who had been a captain in the St Helena Artillery. He kept his Jewish faith, but his second and third wives and all his children were Christians. His brothers and their children moved off, to South Africa and elsewhere, but his own descendants and the Mosses stayed on the island, ran the firm, lived in handsome houses (and had a series of second homes at unfashionable addresses in London), and completed the transformation of their families from Jewish shopkeepers to Christian planter gentry. Saul's daughter-in-law married the Governor of St Helena as her second husband. His grandson, also Saul, married Katherine Welby, daughter of the Bishop of St Helena (and a cousin of Augustus Welby Northmore Pugin). The Solomons owned the first motor car on the island. They must have lived pleasantly enough, even though the death of Napoleon, the opening of the Suez Canal, and new patterns of steamship travel had reduced St Helena to a backwater. Saul's great-grandson Homfray Welby Solomon (known as 'King Sol' on the island) died in 1960. By then he had sold out to a South African company, and the firm is now 84 per cent owned by the government.

Its name survives, however. Martin Drury, just retired from being Director of the National Trust, went there at the end of 2001, and wrote to me about it: 'The name of Solomon is constantly heard at St Helena, and seen everywhere in Jamestown. The business is now known as Solomon and Co., and referred to as Solomon's. Most of the buildings on Main Street, Jamestown, are owned by Solomon's, and display the name on doors and brass plates and shop fascia boards – groceries, clothes, a new hardware/DIY shop, tourist, travel and shipping agency and the Consulate Hotel. It is also the principal landowner on the island and owns and runs many farms. Until the flax industry collapsed in the 1960s Solomon's must have had a large stake in it.'

The Consulate Hotel on the main street of Jamestown was the Solomon residence and, I imagine, also their counting-house and office; it is now one of the two hotels on the island, and its verandah is the resort of St Helena's youth. Next door is the main Solomon warehouse, a fine building of c. 1840. Most of the country houses in St Helena have been eaten by termites, but the Solomons' one, Princess (or Prince's) House, survives, rather crudely restored. Martin brought me back photographs and a plastic shopping-bag with SOLOMONS on it 'to demonstrate that Solomon is still a household name on St Helena'.

Intriguing though the St Helena connection is, what the Solomons and their cousinhood achieved elsewhere, especially in South Africa, is at least as interesting. Three of Nathaniel and Phoebe's grandchildren were, in their different ways and different parts of the world, remarkable: they were Samual Isaac (1815–86), the son of Lewis Isaac of Poole and Catherine Solomon; Nathaniel Isaacs (1808–72), the son of Nathaniel Isaacs of Canterbury and Lenie Solomon; and, most remarkable of all, Saul Solomon (1817–92), the son of Joseph Solomon, of St Helena and Cape Town, and Hannah Moss.

All that I know about Samuel Isaac comes from his short entry in the *Dictionary of National Biography*, which derives entirely from his obituaries in *The Times* and *The Jewish Chronicle*. As a young man he came to London and established a large business as an army contractor, trading along with his brother Saul as Isaac, Campbell and Company. During the American Civil War the firm was the biggest European supporter of the Southern states and, between 1861 and 1865, the most enterprising of blockade runners. Its ships went out loaded with military supplies and returned loaded with cotton. Isaac raised a volunteer regiment from his factory in Northampton (why should Northampton factory workers have wanted to fight in that war?), and was created a major in the Confederate Army. The defeat of the Southern states in 1865 ruined him. By 1880 he had recovered (doing what?) and was in a position to promote the first Mersey tunnel (rail, not road). The tunnel was completed in 1885, and was formally opened by the Prince of Wales in January 1886. 'Queen Victoria accepted from Isaac a jewelled representation of the tunnel, in which the speck of light at the end of the excavation was represented by a brilliant.' He died in the same year, at 29 Warrington Crescent, Maida Vale (down the road from one of my favourite London pubs), leaving £203,084, a considerable sum for those days, and a large collection of pictures by the eminent and largely forgotten Victorian landscape painter B. W. Leader.

His brother, Saul Isaac, must also have made a financial recovery, for he was Conservative MP for Nottingham from 1874 to 1880, and lived in a sizeable country house, Tollerton Hall, a few miles from the town. I imagine he had a factory or business in Nottingham, but know nothing about it.

Nathaniel Isaacs, first cousin of these two brothers, was taken out to St Helena by his uncle Saul Solomon when he was 14, and put to work in the family business. He hated what he called 'the insipidity and monotony of the counting-house'. He had a roving disposition. He signed on on two successive ships which called in at St Helena, and made friends with Lieutenant King, the commander of the second one. With him he sailed in 1826 from Cape Town to look for King's friend Lieutenant Farewell, who had gone on an expedition to East Africa and disappeared. They found him, living miserably and shipless with four other Europeans on the edge of Zulu country, but their own ship was wrecked in the process. They were 400 miles from the nearest English settlement at Algoa Bay (later Port Elizabeth). To keep up their spirits they found it, as Isaacs put it, 'soul stirring and irresistible' to plant an English flag on the sand dunes, next to where Durban was to grow up.

The ship's carpenter started to build a new ship, but it took him two years to complete it. Meanwhile, Nathaniel Isaacs led an extraordinary life, moving between the tiny English settlement and the court of Chaka, the most savage, cruel and formidable of the Zulu kings, whose way it was to have the brains of those who displeased him clubbed out, twenty at a time; Isaacs had to stand by and watch this kind of incident. Chaka took a capricious liking to him, however; sent him on a successful campaign against a neighbouring chief, had his witch doctors administer medicine for his wounds, and ultimately created him a chief and granted him a territory stretching 25 miles along the coast and 100 miles inland. All this happened when Isaacs was aged from 18 to 20 (at which age I was living so much less adventurously in Nigeria).

When the ship was at last in commission, Isaacs agreed to go to Cape Town and try to arrange a treaty between the Zulus and the British government. He failed, but somehow survived Chaka's displeasure up till the latter's death in 1828, when he established good relations with his slightly less ferocious successor, Dingaan. From 1828 to 1833 he was moving between Natal, Cape Town and St Helena, helping to run the little settlement (where sizeable numbers of Africans had put themselves under the settlers' protection) and trying and failing to get the British government interested in the possibilities of developing Natal. A contretemps with Dingaan led to him finally leaving the area in 1833, and he was not involved when, in 1835, the settlers laid out the town of Durban, so named after the Governor in Cape Town, Sir Benjamin d'Urban.

In 1836 he published his *Travels and Adventures in Eastern Africa*. It is a book I know only in extracts, though I am always meaning to call it up in the British Library. It is said to give a vivid and accurate picture of Zulu life and Nathaniel's adventures, even if written in a 'quaintly stilted style'. It was twice reprinted in the last century.

In or soon after its publication, Nathaniel moved to the other side of Africa, and started trading first from Calabar and then from Sierra Leone. European trading stations were only thinly scattered along the West Coast, and had not penetrated inland. In Sierra Leone, it is said that he was 'the only white man within an extensive territory, and became king or ruler of the native tribes'. This was the kind of life that suited him. In partnership with G. C. Redman in London he owned two ships, in which he exported arrowroot and other products to England. He sent his children Ben and Philippa back to England to be educated, and brought out two Lyon cousins (by a Solomon mother) to help him on the West Coast, where they died of fever in 1850. Every few years, up to 1858, he would turn up in Canterbury, where his nephews and nieces enjoyed his stories but not his arrowroot, which he brought with him in large quantities. When the English government began to take an interest in Sierra Leone and questioned his land titles, he moved on yet again and settled on his 'freehold estate called the Island of Matacong' (as he put it in his will) in the Gulf of Guinea. In 1864 he wrote to his cousin Saul Solomon from Liverpool, 'I have been such a rover, and fortune, or change, led me to such out of the way places that I appear, now, like an outcast from that part of the family who were most dear to me in my tender age.' By about 1870 he had retired to Egremont on the Wirral peninsula, a mile or so from where, a few years later, his cousin Samuel Isaac's Mersey tunnel would emerge. He died in 1872.

By then his cousin Saul was at the height of a very different career in South Africa, where the Solomons were now established in increasing numbers. The first member of the family to arrive there had been Benjamin, the brother of Saul the 'Merchant King'. He left St Helena as early as 1806, and for many years was Usher of the Court in Cape Town. He married a Dutch wife, as did most of his children and descendants. They became Christian, as did all the South African Solomons after the first generation. His eldest son, Charles Benjamin, was an architect, and I suspect was the father or more probably grandfather of J. M. Solomon, a gifted young architect who worked as an assistant to Herbert Baker in South Africa and for a time in Lutyens's office in London, and in 1917 was given the commission to build the University of Cape Town, and a superb site on which to build it. He was then living at the Woolsack, the house designed by Baker for

Rudyard Kipling in 1900. Christopher Hussey describes him as 'an architectural idealist . . . full of enthusiasm for the unparalleled site and the great building that he was to design'. Lutyens pronounced his plans 'most excellent', but they were way over budget (not something that ever bothered Lutyens) and 'either the suspense, or the strain of effecting reductions, or the dread that he was unequal to the technical responsibilities, unhinged the architect's mind' and in 1919 (or early 1920?) he committed suicide.

Benjamin Solomon in 1806 was followed by his 12-year-old nephew Saul in 1829, coming from St Helena to study at the South African College at Cape Town, shortly after followed by Saul's parents Joseph and Hannah and the rest of their family.

Saul Solomon was a dwarf. He seems to have been naturally very small, like most of the Solomons, and to have had his growth stopped, his body stunted and his limbs distorted as a result of rheumatic fever wrongly treated when, as a child, he was sent to school for a year or two in England. He is sometimes described as 'the height of a walking-stick'. Anthony Trollope, who saw him speaking in the Cape Colony Assembly, said that he was 'so small that on first seeing him the stranger is certainly impressed with the idea that no man so small has ever been seen by him before.'

He was not deterred by this handicap, and perhaps even stimulated by the need to overcome it. In about 1834, he entered a Cape Town printing works as an apprentice, and quickly rose to become manager and then proprietor of the firm, re-named 'Saul Solomon and Co.' and at one time described, perhaps with exaggeration, as 'the best of its kind on this side of the equator'. It did all the government and most of the private printing in Cape Town, and employed around three hundred people. In 1853 the firm printed the Colony's first postage stamp, the famous Cape Triangular

Blue, issued on 1 September. In 1857 it printed the first issue of what is still one of the main South Africa newspapers, the *Argus*, and in 1863 Saul Solomon became its proprietor (he sold it in 1881). He was also one of the leading businessmen in the growing town, introduced a limited liability law, was chairman of the principal insurance company, and had much to do with the construction of the city harbour and break-water works.

But he is best known as a politician. In 1854 he was elected one of the four members for Cape Town in the first Cape Colony parliament or assembly, and he continued to represent Cape Town until he retired in 1883. When the colony was given responsible government (effectively, made independent) in 1872, he was offered the possibility of becoming the first prime minister; he refused it, and never took office, probably because he thought that his small size, about which he was extremely sensitive, made him unfitted for it. But for 29 years he was one of the dominant personalities in the Parliament. Trollope wrote in 1877: 'I believe that it would hardly be possible to pass any measure of importance through the Cape Legislature to which he offered a strenuous opposition.' He was nicknamed the 'King-maker': 'Ministers rose and fell at his dictation.'

There must have been something at first sight ridiculous about this little monkey (which is what he looked like, until one saw the intelligence of his bright eyes) standing upon a stool so as to be visible to his audience, and spouting Glad-stonian oratory by the hour. When the historian J. A. Froude went to South Africa in 1875 to report on the political situation there to the English government, his first comments on him were condescending: 'In ideas a diminutive John Mill, about as like him and in the same relation to him as the Cape Colony is to England . . . He is the great orator in the Assembly – the size of Tom Thumb – as old as I am and lately married. His wife has produced a baby as big as his male parent.' But over the years, although they differed on many questions, Froude grew to respect and admire him, and in 1886 described him as 'Saul Solomon, one of the best men I know.' And indeed, the more one reads, the more one feels admiration and affection for him – the 'little great man of South Africa'.

In 1880 he showed where his sympathies lay by christening his second son William Ewart Gladstone Solomon. He was a Gladstonian anti-imperialist Liberal, who never deviated from the resolves he announced in 1854: to fight for 'civil and religious liberty' and to oppose 'all legislation tending to introduce distinction, either of class, colour or creed'. He had a vision of a Cape in which English, Dutch, black and coloured people would grow together in civilisation and prosperity – and, beyond that, to a federation of like minds and states in South Africa. He was inevitably attacked at the time as a 'negrophilist'. In the Cape (in part due to him, I think, and in contrast to the rest of British and Dutch South Africa) anyone – white, Indian, black or coloured – who reached the requisite property qualification had the right to vote, and Saul resisted any attempt to attack this right; it was not until 1885, after he had left politics, that the first reduction in the black and coloured franchise took place, and not until 1948 that it was finally extinguished. Saul fought, too, long and hard for justice for the native tribes on the Cape frontiers, Basutos, Zulus and Griquas. When he died, *Imvo*, the Native newspaper, issued a full-page portrait of him to its subscribers, and called him 'the most able, unflinching, and unswerving champion of justice to Natives that this land has ever known'.

Almost all my paternal forebears have been visual philistines, but Saul must have had a certain sense of style; at least Clarensville, his house at Sea Point three miles outside

Cape Town, was an agreeable contrast to Quatre Vents, my
Girouard great-grandfather's villa outside Montreal. It was
bought not built by him, and said to have been the work of a
'Frenchman', perhaps the able neo-classical architect Louis-
Michel Thibault, who was in practice at Cape Town between
1783 and about 1810. It was a single-storey house, which
was convenient for Saul, but very spacious. The main feature
was its long and lofty Tuscan portico (a 'noble stoep', Saul
called it), which ran along the front of the house. Behind rose
the spur of Table Mountain known as the Lion's Head. In
front was a wide vista of beach, rocks, the Atlantic, and the
silhouette of Robben Island in the distance.

Saul made a luxuriant garden at Clarensville. Its central
feature was a pond, crossed by a bridge, scattered with fountains, and overhung by weeping willows, with finches' nests
dangling from their boughs; the goldfish that filled it recognised the tap of his little walking stick on the bridge and rose
to the surface to be fed by him. In addition to the finches there
were peacocks, pigeons, magpies, a mocking-bird and a secretary bird, which stalked around the grounds and was adopted
by Saul as his crest.

Other features were described in a letter from his wife to
her father:

> You would be pleased with our cows, pigs, poultry, etc.
> in which our new gardener takes great pride. He is a
> sort of steward – such a genius too – a splendid musi-
> cian – plays all the classical music. Saul has allowed
> him to fit up a pretty sitting room and bedroom off it in
> our great yard, or rather court, for it is large enough
> for a sort of baronial residence, and we have given him
> our harmonium, and he plays on it so exquisitely. On
> Sunday mornings when Saul and I go up to walk on the
> terrace, and sit on the bridge over the water-lily pond

with the lovely creepers overhead – the goldfish sporting below and the little fountains playing, we are generally serenaded by Mr Roberts, who plays his best sacred music, and it sounds so sweetly in the distance, blending with the murmur of the waves on the shore.

Saul was extremely hospitable, and loved meeting people, so that there was a great deal of coming and going at Clarensville – from swarms of children to David Livingstone, General Gordon, J. A. Froude and Princes Edward and George (later George V) on tour in 1860, the former 'anxious to please his illustrious grandmother, who told him to discuss politics and learn the facts from the great man, Mr Saul Solomon'.

The heart of the house was the large library, where Saul would sit under portraits of Cromwell and Milton in the early hours of the morning and late into the evening (he only took four hours' sleep), reading, making notes, writing letters, and equipping himself to become far and away the best-informed person in the Cape Parliament. Froude loved the library, and enjoyed browsing in it. 'I never tire of reading here,' he remarked, 'the interesting history of a comprehensive and many-sided mind.' I own just one work from it, a bulky two-volume edition of the writings of Edmund Burke, with a book-plate as small as its owner: 'Saul Solomon, Cape Town', and an inscription from his widow to my great-grandfather, 'In memory of S.S.'

It was near Clarensville, in a newly made reservoir, that Saul's little daughter Maggie drowned in 1881. Her governess, who jumped in to rescue her in full Victorian dress, drowned too. Saul never really recovered. The great Zulu chief Cetewayo, then a prisoner after the Zulu War (of which Saul strongly disapproved), sent him a moving letter of condolence: 'I am writing to my great friend Mr Saul Solomon to express my deep sorrow at the very great misfortune that has come down on your house. I feel so very sorry to hear that one of your branches has withered and left you. I really do not know how to express my great sorrow as touching such a great calamity.'

The last years of Saul's life after his daughter's death were sad ones. In 1883 he had a nervous breakdown, and his doctors sent him to England for two years to recuperate (he had taken a sea trip to England in 1863 to help him recover from 'miserable depression'; I imagine the strain imposed by his deformity must have been considerable). On his return in 1885 he found that his two nephews, to whom he had handed over the management of Saul Solomon and Company, had reduced it to insolvency, and he had lost most of his money. In 1886 his brother Edward drowned when staying at Clarensville. In 1888 he and his family left South Africa for England and for good. In 1889 George, the youngest of his three sons, died of blood poisoning, aged 11. He himself died in 1892, after three years of often excruciating pain, bravely borne, from a kidney disease compounded by rheumatism and heart trouble. As I have a taste for cemeteries, one of these days I may make my way to his grave in the Ocklynge Cemetery in Eastbourne (but I don't like Eastbourne). The inscription on it reads in part: 'The memory of his noble life dedicated from boyhood to the service of Christ and human-ity remains a benediction for South Africa.' Remarkable though the Solomons were as a family, he is the only member of it who had a touch of greatness. I wish I was directly descended from him, rather than from his missionary brother Edward, admirable man and loyal supporter of Saul though the latter was.

Saul's Scottish wife, Georgiana Thomson, was a fighter like her husband. In her widowhood she removed to London where she 'actively participated in the affairs of the Josephine

Butler Society, the Women's Freedom League, the Anti-Slavery and Aborigines' Society, the Suffragette Fellowship, the British Commonwealth League, and numerous other social and political organisations'. In 1912, when leading a suffragette demonstration to Parliament, aged 68, she resisted the police, was arrested and spent a month in Holloway Gaol. In the South African War her sympathies were on the side of the Boers, and after the war she went out to the Transvaal to help in the rehabilitation of Boer women and children. She died in 1933. Her daughter Daisy lived with her in London, was also a suffragette, and also did her time in Holloway: she was picked up by a policeman outside Parliament and removed bodily ('not a very difficult feat considering that she was very slight and less than five feet in height', according to one account).

Saul's elder son, also Saul, moved from being a barrister to serving as a Church of England clergyman in the East End of London, but then converted to Catholicism, went back to South Africa and the law, and after a successful career ended up a judge. He has a claim to be the only man who married a couple as a clergyman and divorced them as a judge. His brother William Ewart Gladstone was uninfluenced by his name and never showed the slightest interest in politics. He became a painter, trained at the Royal Academy Schools in London, and was first Principal and then Director of the Government School of Art in Bombay. I like to think that he spent twenty years persuading his students to abandon their Indian traditions and paint in the style of Sargent; but I may be maligning him. He had considerable facility. I own his portrait of my grandmother, or to be exact half of it. It was originally a full-length, but my father considered it slick, vulgar and (I think) not a good likeness, and cut off the bottom half, to reduce it to manageable size.

Mary Solomon, the daughter of the dwarf Saul's brother Henry, is the only other Solomon to have had a proper book published about her: *Mrs John Brown, 1847–1935*, edited by Angela James and Nina Hills, and published by John Murray in 1935. Its most interesting part is her reminiscences of life as a GP's wife in the mill- and coal-mining town of Burnley in Lancashire between 1879 and 1898 (her husband was a cousin of Dr John Brown of Edinburgh, famous in Victorian days for his dog-story *Rab and his Friends*). They lived over the consulting room in the centre of the town, and from their drawing-room window could count 100 factory chimneys belching smoke. Every morning at 5.30 they were woken up by the 'immense rattle' of clogs on paving-stones, as the mill-hands went to work. 'Who can forget it . . . who could *wish* to forget it? Not I. It thrills me still!'

She was small, generous-hearted and fearless, and launched into any aspect of Burnley life where she thought she could help, or was asked to help. She ran a Sunday School for mill girls; a discussion group for mill-hands in her drawing-room; joined the Co-op and started up a Burnley Co-Operative Women's Guild; visited the workhouse; gave talks to the police; walked or went on the milk cart three miles up into the bleak hills once a week to talk, pray and eat with the navvies who were building a reservoir there and had no one to take an interest in them; started up a rescue home for girls; and had to stay a succession of lecturers with little money for hotels, or with a good cause: General Booth of the Salvation Army, Lady Henry Somerset, the crusading queen of temperance, Eleanor Aveling, Karl Marx's daughter, and many others. Though never a party member, she was attracted to socialism, and became a friend of Keir Hardie and Edward Carpenter.

There are various glimpses of, or stories about, her that

appeal to me. A deputation of young mill-hands came to see her and said, 'There are girls that work in our mills that we call Mrs Doctor Brown's disciples. They are *different*, and it is all because of you. We want you to come in and speak to us young men that we may be better company for them girls.'

She attended a sceptical all-male meeting of the Co-Operative Society to speak up for women, and their need to have access to the library, reading room and lectures like the men. They made her get up on a chair – 'Get on t'cheer. We's cannot see yo.' So she did, and made her speech, and persuaded them.

Her sex, small size and courage aroused a protective streak in working-class men in Burnley. When there was a miners' strike in 1892 (she was on the Relief Committee, which helped families in the distress of a long lock-out) and she attended a public meeting in the cattle-market at Burnley, willing hands lifted her on to a wagon so that she could get a view. There were always a couple of devoted mill-hands or navvies ready to go round with her as guards or escorts. But when a huge drunken navvy came into one of her meetings and made a disturbance, she wouldn't let the men touch him, but walked straight up to him and chucked him out herself – the story went round the town.

I like to think of her reading Walt Whitman (propped open on the mantelpiece) as she did the dusting, and being the first woman in Burnley to ride a bicycle; and am moved by the story of the two prostitutes who called to ask her to come with them to see a young mill-hand who was dying in their lodgings and asking for her – she went immediately.

She was so interested in and sympathetic to individual people and their problems that I don't think she was ever found intrusive, as a do-gooder thinking in abstractions might have been. Her navvies, after she had spent some weeks bringing them up food in the milk-cart when there was no work or pay at the reservoir due to frost, unharnessed the horse and pulled her with cheers down to town themselves when the frost was over. When, in 1894, women were at last declared eligible for election as Poor Law Guardians, she stood in Burnley and, without any canvassing on her part, was elected at the head of the poll by a predominantly working-class vote. She was now an overseer of the work-house and, though she disliked the system, she worked hard to make it more humane – for instance, getting rid of the regulation by which old married couples were separated into male and female wards.

In her first year at Burnley a bulky package arrived in the post, containing an ill-written, much erased manuscript wrapped in a piece of canvas smelling of African wood-smoke. It was the manuscript of *The Story of an African Farm*, sent to her by Olive Schreiner, her great friend in South Africa. By finding a reader, she helped to get it published, and it was ultimately dedicated to her. She was criticised for accepting the dedication (as she was for much else that was considered unsuitable for a nicely brought-up lady) because the book caused a furore on publication, and indignant mothers put it on the fire to keep it from sullying their daughters – something hard to understand when one reads it today.

Edward Solomon, her uncle and my great-great-grandfather, was born in St Helena on 25 December 1820, and held up as a baby to see Napoleon lying in state. Like his brother Saul and possibly also his brother Henry he was educated at the South African College in Cape Town. I own the small copy of Cicero's *De Officiis*, nicely bound in gilt-tooled leather, that he won as a prize for progress in Latin letters in August 1831, when he was aged only ten. A bookplate states that it is a prize from 'Athenaeo Austro Africano, Promontorii Bonae Spei' and carries five signatures, of members of the staff or board of governors. One of them is of James Rose

Innes, who taught mathematics at the College, whose son and grandson were to be close friends of the Solomons, and whose great-granddaughter Dorothy was to be one of the brides-maids at my grandparents' wedding in Pretoria in 1903. Two years later she married Helmuth von Moltke, son of the Prussian Field-Marshal; her son, also Helmuth, was executed by Hitler in 1945.

I also own a copy (sent to my father in 1924) of the letter that Edward Solomon wrote to a friend on 15 August 1835, describing the stages of his conversion to Christianity. He seems, in fact, to have had little teaching from his nominally Jewish parents, or anyone else of the Jewish faith. He served for eighteen years or so (like David Livingstone and Robert Moffat) as one of the London Missionary Society's African missionaries. He worked with the Griquas and Basutos in then remote country – for diamonds had not yet been found at Kimberley – at Philippolis, Fauresmith and Griquatown, several weeks by ox-wagon from Cape Town. In 1857, he left the missions because of his wife's health, and from then until 1884 was Pastor of the English church at Bedford in Cape Colony. He was one of Saul's main sources of information on native affairs, and 'an uncompromising advocate for even-handed justice to Black and White alike'. He drowned, as already related, near Clarensville in 1886.

In connection with Edward I can't resist saying something about Martha Solomon, marginal though she is to the story. She was a black woman or girl who, my father told me, was given her surname when Edward converted or baptised her or both. This was not unusual at the time, apparently. She took up with and finally married an Englishman called Harry Grey, who had come out to South Africa and failed to make good. In 1883 he inherited the title of Earl of Stamford and a big estate from a distant cousin. My friend Rupert Gunnis had a story about the rather starchy family solicitor, who went out to South Africa to inform him of his good fortune. With some difficulty he ran him to earth in a shanty somewhere, and delivered his message. Then he pompously added, 'And may I venture to ask if there is a young heir to bear the historic title of Lord Grey of Groby?' 'Come here, Jack,' shouted the new Earl, and a coal-black piccaninny came trotting through the door. In fact it turned out that he had been born before the marriage, so he never made the House of Lords, but an equally black daughter was born after it. I always thought that she was called Lady Jane Grey, but I see on looking at the Peerage that she was Lady Mary Grey.

Edward also married a Scottish wife, Jessie Matthews. They had eight children, four of whom had distinguished careers: Sir Edward, Sir William, Sir Richard and the youngest child, Emilie.

Emilie (1858–1939 or 1940), besides being Principal of a girls' high school, a suffragette and supporter of the native vote, had a public career not unlike that of her aunt Georgiana and her cousin Mary Brown. She was a founder member of the Cape Town Temperance Union, and later President of the Cape Province Temperance Union and Vice-President of the World Christian Temperance Union, in which capacity she travelled indefatigably round the world. She was Founder and First President of the Congregational Women's Federation of South Africa, Chairman of the Peninsula Church Council of the Congrational Church and (aged 76) first woman Chairman of the Congregational Union of South Africa. She was Vice-President of the South African National Council of Women. This is all a bit daunting; yet she was clearly not a grim-faced killjoy but jolly, friendly, broad-minded, and loved jokes and giving parties. I imagine that, like quite a few Temperance advocates, she was born one over par, and had no need of stimulants. Field-Marshal Smuts called her 'the pick of the bunch of her distinguished family'.

My father described her as 'very plump in a firm, compact way, with a large bosom and a broad behind. For years she had a heavy moustache and nascent beard'. He once told me that when she found out that she could have treatment for her facial hair, and looked into the mirror for the first time after it had been successfully removed, she burst into tears.

Of her three knighted brothers Edward, the eldest (in full, Edward Philip Solomon, 1845–1914) became head of the leading firm of solicitors in Johannesburg. He was one of the supporters of the Jameson Raid, was arrested, put briefly in a Pretoria gaol, and ultimately fined £2000. After the Boer War he went into politics, served as Minister of Works in the Transvaal government, and became a senator after union in 1910. His brother William (1850–1930) never got involved in politics but kept to the law, first as a barrister and then, from 1887, as a judge. From 1928 to 1930 he was Chief Justice of South Africa, in succession to his friend James Rose-Innes. He retired in 1930, having been a judge for 43 years, and died in the same year. As he lived on after his brothers our father got to know him well, liked him very much and respected him for his gentle way of telling him off with a quiet question: 'You don't think it is better to live within your income?' 'Do you think you might help him?' and so on. In a letter to me he describes how 'he dressed quietly, neatly and expensively. He was very reserved and lacked vitality but liked pretty women, especially large Rubens types, good food, wine in modest quantities, foreign travel and quiet conviviality.'

Like his brother, Richard Solomon was sent to the South African College in Cape Town, and on to Peterhouse in Cambridge, paid for by his uncle Saul. He read law at the Inner Temple, and then went back to the Cape to practise as a barrister. In 1881 he married Mary Walton, daughter of the Wesleyan Minister in Grahamstown. I have his letter of proposal:

My dear Miss Polly

I see no opportunity of having a talk with you so I am forced to write instead. I have seen Mr Walton and therefore I am not breaking the ordinary rules of society. The fact of the matter is I have learned to love you and I am bold enough to ask you whether you will return that love. I feel that with you I have a very bright future, while without you it will be a perfect blank. I am confident that with your assistance I shall rise to the highest position in my profession, and without you I believe I shall end in failure. Please let me have a reply today, one word will be sufficient if that word be yes . . .

She did say yes, and he did rise. He became a successful barrister, and when he joined the Kimberley bar scooped out a great plum: he won the De Beers retainer. He was now the barrister representing Cecil Rhodes and Alfred Beit, the rand multi-millionaires. He acted for Rhodes at the time of the Jameson Raid, though I doubt if he approved of it. It seems to his credit that he then fell out with him and lost the retainer. I would like to believe the story that Rhodes said, 'Solomon is the one man I cannot bribe,' but my father was doubtful of it – though Rhodes certainly bribed many people, and Richard Solomon would not have been one of them. Anyway, in 1898 he became Attorney-General of the Cape under W. O. Schreiner, brother of Olive, in the tradition of Saul Solomon (as Rhodes certainly was not) in his attitude to the natives, and his desire to work out a compromise to avoid war with the Boer republics. He failed, and in June 1900, a year after the South African War started, his government fell.

My great-grandfather went off to England for a time, and came back when the war had reached the point where the British army had occupied the Transvaal and Orange Free

State, and Milner had been appointed the administrator of the conquered republics. He was appointed legal adviser to the Transvaal administration under Milner, and to Kitchener, as Commander-in-Chief, during the last stages of the war. In May 1902, when the Boers were becoming desperate, English and Boer delegates, my great-grandfather among them, assembled at Vereeniging to discuss and attempt to come to agreement about peace terms. Among the photograph albums which belonged to my father (all too few and faded), I have some evocative panoramic photographs of the scattering of tents and marquees on the huge empty veldt at Vereeniging, and the huddle of English and Dutch delegates standing with their hangers-on outside the largest of them, in which discussions took place.

Peace was finally concluded on 31 May; the final wording had been worked out by Milner, Solomon, Smuts and Herzog. I used to own the pen with which (so an inscription on the box which held it claimed) the peace had been signed. I imagine that several pens were, in fact, involved. I gave my one to Thomas Pakenham, as encouragement when he was starting work on his book on the Boer War. It was an ordinary red wooden push-pen, such as used to be issued to us at my preparatory school, remarkably unimpressive for the occasion.

Among the clauses of the peace was what became the famous or infamous Clause 9. The fact that native and coloured people had voting rights (however hedged with restrictions) in the Cape, and none at all in the Dutch republics, had been one of the issues of the war; something had to be said about it in the peace. It had been agreed that, after an interval, responsible government would be restored to the defeated republics. Clause 9 (agreed to as a concession to the Boers) stated that consideration of the question of granting votes to 'natives' would be deferred until 'after' the introduction of responsible government, that is to say it would be left to their governments as then elected. Everyone involved knew that this meant that the natives would not get voting rights, as inevitably turned out to be the case; and after the Union had taken place in 1909, the Dutch majority was used to bring the Cape, bit by bit, in line with the rest; the last shreds of a non-white Cape vote went in 1948. I wish my great-grandfather had not been associated with this clause.

For the next five years, until responsible government was introduced in 1906–7, the Transvaal was run under an appointed assembly and an inner group or 'cabinet', led by Milner. The Solomons' friend James Rose Innes was Chief Justice; William Solomon was First Puisne Justice; and Richard Solomon became Attorney-General, Leader of the Assembly, and for a considerable time acting Lieutenant-Governor. In these years he continued to remodel the Statute Law of the Transvaal; as remodelled, it was adopted under responsible government, and became the basis of the Statute Law of the Union. These were responsible and busy years for him: he was a big man in Pretoria, and in 1903, when his daughter married my grandfather (then head of the Transvaal railways), the marriage was a great occasion and the daughter of the Chief Justice and the two daughters of the Commander-in-Chief were among the bridesmaids. I have a yellowing page of a Pretoria newspaper describing the event and dresses in detail, and listing all the presents. A special train, gaily decorated with Union Jacks, conveyed the couple down to Cape Town, where they spent their honeymoon in Cecil Rhodes's house, Groote Schuur.

In these years Richard drew away from Milner, who left South Africa in 1905. Milner had no love for the Afrikaners; his ambition, which never came near realisation, was to bring in sufficient British settlers to destroy the Boer majority in the Transvaal. Richard was by nature a bridger of gulfs; he wanted Dutch and English to come together, and forget the past. When responsible government came in 1907 (earlier than Milner wanted it to come), he and his brother Edward formed a party which fought the first election jointly with the Dutch Het Volk party, against the 'Progressives', the English disciples of Rhodes and Milner. The Dutch leaders needed their support and accepted, not too happily, that if the coalition won they would serve under Richard Solomon as the first Prime Minister of the Transvaal in the new dispensation.

But his past association with Milner put him in an awkward position. The Progressives reviled him as a traitor; Rudyard Kipling, Milner's friend and admirer, attacked him as 'one Sir Richard Solomon, a sort of political pimp and go-between who has been in Milner's administration, but who is capable of doing anything and everything that might lead to his own advancement.' But the Het Volk party only grudgingly accepted him as a potential leader. As Smuts put it, 'You cannot be chief henchman to Milner and aspire to be saviour of South Africa.'

While he was on a visit to England, Smuts and others nominated him to stand in the election against the charismatic Progressive Sir Percy Fitzpatrick (whose *Jock of the Bushveld* was in every schoolroom and school library when I was young), in the deliberate hope that he would lose. He did lose. The coalition won the election, but Botha, not Solomon, became the first Prime Minister of the Transvaal, and went on to become the first Prime Minister of the Union. Edward Solomon was given the post of Minister of Works; Richard went off to England as the Agent-General for the Transvaal, and remained to serve as High Commissioner for the Union, until his early and sudden death in November 1913.

There was never to be an English (as opposed to Dutch) Prime Minister of the Transvaal, let alone of the Union. If (as was so very much on the cards) Richard Solomon had got the job instead of Botha, would things have worked out differently? Would he have become the first Prime Minister of the Union? It does not seem likely, because of the kind of person he was. His record – for Rhodes, against Rhodes, for Milner against the Dutch, for the Dutch against Milner – seems to bear out the damning criticism of Merriman, the Prime Minister of the Cape, that he 'is never certain, from one moment to the next, what his opinion is!' One of his obituaries wrote more sympathetically of his being 'perhaps too honest and too changeable, too eager and too impulsive, to make a good politician'. Temperamentally, he was an enabler, not a leader. The post of High Commissioner suited him very well; he established an excellent relationship with Botha and Smuts, and did valuable work to create good relations between English and Dutch in South Africa and between the South African and British governments (the natives had been forgotten; at the time of the Union Schreiner came to England to plead their cause, and could not get a serious hearing). When he died all the flags in Cape Town were lowered to half-mast.

Since my father was his only grandchild and ultimately his heir, I own a good many bits and pieces to do with him. I have a smallish and very miscellaneous collection of papers, part political, part personal, including the menu of a dinner that he gave for my grandfather, signed by, amongst others, Asquith, Churchill, Smuts and Botha, and a long letter to him from Lord Curzon, in his own huge handwriting, apologising for his not having been sufficiently well looked after at the great Durbar of 1903. I have a bronze head of him by Derwent Wood, a version of the one on his memorial in the chapel at Peterhouse, and all his many medals and orders, including the impressive chain of a GCMG. My great-grandmother had these mounted and framed for me, but in a foolish moment I demounted them to wear at a fancy-dress party, and they are now bundled up at the back of a drawer. I used to have a set of crystal reproductions of the many stones cut from the Cullinan Diamond which, as Agent-General, he presented to George V in 1907 – but they were stolen, I suspect by a magpie cleaning lady. I still wear his gold cuff-links, engraved with his monogram. My favorite memento of him is a little rococo-style medal, with his name engraved on the back, and on the front an embossed engine puffing smoke and the inscription 'South African Railways. Life Pass'. When he died the stationmaster of Johannesburg wrote to his widow of how he was 'much loved, honoured and respected here amongst railway officials for his lovable and unostentatious demeanour at all times'.

He was clearly a very nice man. And yet I have never been able to empathise with him, or find him interesting, as I do so many of the other Solomons, or his son-in-law, my grandfather.

14

My grandparents

I WAS FIRST made aware of my grandfather at my day-school in South Kensington – St Philip's, familiarly known as 'Mr Tibbits' from its headmaster and proprietor. I was about seven, and we were in class, being read extracts from *The River War*, Winston Churchill's account of taking part in Kitchener's expedition to conquer the Mahdi and avenge Gordon. Why this was considered suitable for seven-year-old boys I can't think – but after all, why not? Anyway, we got to the passage where Churchill wrote about my grandfather and how he built the desert railway for Kitchener – I quote a bit: 'Eminent railway engineers and distinguished soldiers' had said:

> it was impossible to construct such a line . . . It is scarcely within the power of words to describe the savage desolation of the regions into which the line and its construction plunged . . . Lieutenant Girouard, to whom everything was entrusted, was told to make the necessary estimates. Sitting in his hut at Wadi Halfa, he drew up a comprehensive list. Nothing was forgotten. Every want was provided for; every difficulty was foreseen; every requisite was noted. The questions to be decided were numerous and involved. 'How much carrying capacity was required? How much rolling stock? How many engines? What spare parts? How much oil? How many lathes? How many cutters? How

many punching and shearing machines . . . How many miles of rail? How many thousand sleepers?' Such was the comprehensive accuracy of the estimate that the working parties were never delayed by the want even of a piece of brass wire.

And the master said, 'This is about Girouard's grand-father, boys,' or something like that, and I can remember preening myself with my five minutes of reflected glory.

The Sudan War was indeed his finest hour – when the railway, the vital link to convey the British expedition to Khartoum, was built across burning desert, bridges over ravines and all, faster than a railway had ever been built before, by the 'band of boys', young sapper officers in their twenties with, at their head, 29-year-old Lieutenant Girouard, the brash French-Canadian from Kingston Mili-tary Academy, Ontario, who dared to be cheeky to Kitchener, and whom Kitchener thought the world of – and afterwards put at the head of Egyptian Railways, enabling G. W. Steevens, in his bestselling *With Kitchener to Khartoum*, to describe 'the crowning wonder of British Egypt – a subaltern with all but Cabinet rank and £2000 a year'. (I own a sheet of paper covered with elaborate Arabic script, which I think is creating him Girouard Bimbashi – the rank below that of Girouard Pasha, which he would probably have attained too if he had not been taken away from Egypt by the Boer War).

I didn't think much more about my grandfather until I bumped into him again, so to speak, thirteen years or so later, when I was a National Service subaltern at Kaduna in Northern Nigeria (purely by chance or, perhaps one should say, incompetence, for those who only just scraped through to a commission tended to be sent to remote places where it was thought they could do no harm). The silver brought out for the officers on mess nights included a cup, slightly lop-sided and dented – the result, perhaps, of high jinks on previous mess nights – which had been presented by Sir E. P. C. Girouard to my battalion of the Nigeria Regiment (his own party piece on mess nights and festive occasions was singing 'Alouette'). My connection with him got talked about a little, I suppose; anyway, on the strength of it I was asked to breakfast with the – not District Officer, he was a grade up from that – whatever-he-was of Kaduna, in his official residence. He was a shyish man, and there were only the two of us at breakfast; afterwards he took me to look at a framed photograph of Sir Percy – we gazed at it in silence, for neither of us could think of anything to say.

It was railways which had brought my grandfather to Nigeria after running and remodelling, with success, Egyptian Railways, and being taken away from them to run the railways in the Boer War and to rebuild them as quickly as the Boers blew them up – hence a knighthood, at the age of 33 – and then, after the peace, being put in charge of railways in the Transvaal. There he married my grandmother, but was pushed out of his job by the mining lobby in Johannesburg on the grounds that a businessman was needed, not a soldier. But he was then taken up by Winston Churchill, who had not forgotten him, and sent to Northern Nigeria, first as High Commissioner, then as Governor, primarily to build a railway there – which he did, but he did much else as well.

I don't think I knew much about this at the time, and in succeeding years I still had little sympathy with him. He was just a man with a monocle – an empire builder, no doubt, but not someone I could relate to, or feel I would like to have known.

My feelings changed when, a few years before my father's death, I got to read the letters which he had written from Africa to my father, then aged five, I think. I had long known about these letters, and how much my father had enjoyed them at the time, but he thought that he had lost them. They turned up, however, in some papers that I took to sort and store for him. There are all too few of them – twelve from Nigeria and one from Kenya, where he was Governor after Nigeria. He wrote in capitals and interspersed the text with vivid little drawings of his life and adventures in Africa. They are delightful letters, funny and human, infused with a great sense of the ridiculous, and full of affection for 'Dear Dicky', 'Dear Dickywick', 'My dear Sunboy'. He came alive to me, and I liked him.

The last letter, from Kenya, has a sketch of my grandmother, perched cross-legged with her gun on top of a dead buffalo: 'Dear Dicky, here are some pictures of your mummy slaying a buffalo. She is very proud of what she has done. Such a very small mummy and such a very big buffalo.'

My father's papers also included a large collection of his mother's letters to her parents, mostly from Kenya, giving her own account of life at Government House, of how she redecorated it and entertained in it, of the settler community, her exploits as a big game hunter, etc. (her trophy heads line, or used to line, the walls of a Sandwich golf club; I had one of her lion skins as a rug in my room at Ampleforth, until the matron threw it out). She had stayed in England when my grandfather went out to Nigeria – my father thought that this was when their marriage started to go wrong. She only went to Kenya for two five-month visits, leaving my father behind with his grandparents; she had been persuaded to go by her father, and had promised him to behave while she was out there. But the tensions between them emerge clearly enough in her letters. On her first visit she travelled out from England with her young cousin Anna Walton and Bobby Oppenheim, a cavalry subaltern who had been ill, and was going out to Kenya to stay at Government House and recuperate. They all went on safari together, and her letters are full of him.

My grandfather had been brought in to Kenya to replace a disastrously weak Governor. He was very much a strong one, independent and impatient of Colonial Office control; he re-organised the administration, established good (some said, too good) relations with the settlers, and made the colony financially self-sufficient, an achievement of which he was rightly proud. The most controversial feature of his governor-ship was his moving of the great Masai tribe to concentrate them in one reserve, something the rights and wrongs of which are still debated. He left Kenya at the end of 1912, to take up a major post as one of the managing directors of Armstrong Whitworth's, the great armaments manufacturers. He had been headhunted for this, and as for some time he had felt increasingly frustrated by the Colonial Office, and the Colonial Office increasingly irritated by him, the post (more remunerative than his governorship) came as a useful way out for both parties. He returned to England, and entered on his new work with enthusiasm and success. But the marriage got no better; and after the death of Richard Solomon in 1913 my grandmother asked for a divorce, which was granted in June 1914. In April 1915 she went out to Egypt to marry Bobby Oppenheim, who was there with his regiment, waiting to go to Gallipoli. She returned to England, pregnant with twins, at the end of 1915, and she and the twins died at Budleigh Salterton, where she had rented a house, shortly after their birth on 16 May 1916.

For me, the revelation of reading my grandfather's letters from Nigeria was followed, a few years later, by the deeply moving experience of reading the letters that he wrote to his niece, Virginia Skynner, in the last years of his life. I found both lots of letters so much more sympathetic than my grand-mother's, lively though these are, that, having been previously, if anything, on her side, I transferred my loyalties to my grandfather, and wrote her off as conventional, spoilt and snobbish. Well, I don't know. They were, at the least, ill-suited to each other.

My grandmother had been sent over from South Africa to go to school in England at Wycombe Abbey, in its earliest days as a school. She was much liked, and known as 'Twinkle', I imagine because of her bright eyes (I owe the nickname to a letter written when she died by her school-friend Winifred Knox, sister of Ronald). She was small, like all the Solomons; my father used to say that she was not conventionally pretty, but attractive because of her vitality. She was physically brave and adept, good at all sports, a bold rider, a big game hunter when it was still unusual for women to do more than follow the guns. It must have been enjoyable for the settler community to have this lively 27-year-old as the Governor's wife, even if only part-time, instead of some tough old matron. She was the only child of adoring parents, and spoilt as a result – and extravagant, one of the sources of stress in the marriage. She was a chain-smoker – at least, Sylvia Chancellor and her sisters, when they were young women, were told by the old family nanny: 'If you go on smoking like that, you'll die in childbirth, like Lady Girouard.' She had nothing at all of the do-gooding, radical, suffragette streak of her relatives. She was snobbish, perhaps – not blatantly so, as her mother may have been, but feeling that the world of country houses and nice people was the world to which she belonged, or would like to belong.

But her husband was a brash colonial, not an English gentleman, or desirous of becoming one. There was a bravado and swagger in the way he came into a room, voice raucous, eye-glass flashing (he used it as a weapon, people said), which must increasingly have grated on her once the first glamour of his reputation had worn off. I doubt if she enjoyed his renderings of 'Alouette'. My impression is that he remained in love with her, and that the anger and bad temper of which she complained were a product of the hurt which he felt in being kept at a distance by her (one of their rows in Kenya was because she did not have his photograph on her dressing-table – they had separate bedrooms, incidentally). I may be quite wrong about this – there is so little to go on. I always regret that, having met and liked Anna Reed (as Anna Walton became) at a family funeral, I did not go back to talk to her, especially about the time she spent in Kenya with my grandparents – she could have told me a lot. When she died this is what my grandfather wrote to her mother:

> God knows how much I feel in this dreadful tragedy of life for I cared, Mary, Oh! How I cared and loved, it was not for me to satisfy her in this life though I had hoped for much with little Dick. I was hard, unthinking, careless at times, but I loved her and it is hard to think that we never may meet again on this side of eternity.
>
> Rambling thoughts of her past have been with me all these days and she came to me often as she has done in my dreams as my 'po' lil Gwen', my darling little woman I was unworthy of – She cared, I loved.

I should say something about Bobby Oppenheim and his family. The Oppenheims were Christianised Jews, like the Solomons, but socially and financially better established, at any rate in England. Bobby Oppenheim's father Henry was one of the Jewish financiers to whom Edward VII took a liking when he was Prince of Wales, and brought into society. He married an Anglo-Irish wife of good family, Isabella Butler. They had a house just outside Windsor, and in London lived at 16 Bruton Street, off Berkeley Square, next to the house of Lord and Lady Strathmore, where the Queen Mother was born. Here Henry Oppenheim built up a fine art collection, and he and his wife entertained much and with discrimination. 'As a member of the Turf, Marlborough, St James and White's,' as his *Times* obituary put it, 'he was a well-known figure and his house became a rendezvous of artists, literary men and politicians'. He left around £700,000 when he died in 1912. Of this at least £100,000 must have come to Bobby Oppenheim, in addition to whatever he may have been given before his father died – enough for him and our grandmother to live on very comfortably in those days. He had been to Eton, I think, and was a member of White's, like all his family. His best friend, and the best man at the wedding, was the charismatic and immensely rich Lord Howard de Walden. All of this would have appealed to our grandmother; and perhaps their shared Jewish blood (he one half, she one quarter) was also a link, consciously or unconsciously.

In addition, and perhaps above all, he was clearly a charming man. My father always spoke of him with affection; and Lord Howard de Walden's son pays a glowing tribute to him in his autobiography. He fell in love with my grandmother and waited patiently for six years till he could marry her. 'I love him more than I thought it was possible to love anyone,' she wrote from Egypt. 'It's my first taste of happiness, and every moment is precious to me.'

At the beginning of the 1914–18 war my grandfather carried a good deal of weight. In addition to his past reputation (to which Mount Girouard in the Rockies and Girouard Avenue in Nairobi bore witness), he was, as vice-chairman, to a large extent running one of the nation's two great commercial armaments manufacturers – for Sir Andrew Noble, the chairman, was in retirement, and no longer involved in the business. He was at the prime of life, aged 48, and still bursting with energy.

In the very first days of the war he took part in a small bit of history-making. On 1 August, three days before war was declared, he had been with Kitchener at his country house in Kent, having gone down to see him before he left to return to Egypt where he was Agent and Consul-General – effectively its ruler, like Cromer before him. They had discussed the confusion that was reigning at the War Office. Then, on 2 August, my grandfather had gone into Brooks's, looked into the small front room and seen there Austen Chamberlain, Lord Lansdowne, Victor Cavendish (Aunt Evie's husband), Bonar Law and Edward Carson in close discussion together. He moved on to the smoking-room, but seeing his friend Leverton Harris, a Conservative MP, coming into the club (my father, by the way, thought that he had had an affair with Harris's wife), he guessed that he was going to join the others, stopped him in the hall, expostulated on the situation at the War Office, and suggested that Kitchener was the man to sort it out – but that he was about to leave the country. Leverton Harris passed on his views and, according to Austen Chamberlain, 'this idea was taken up', and Asquith approved it. On 3 August, Kitchener was caught at Dover when already on board ship and about to sail, brought back to London, and appointed Secretary of State for War on 5 August. The famous poster was issued shortly afterwards.

One of my most poignant possessions is a thick 'Instanter Newspaper Scrapbook' crammed with press cuttings covering events to do with munitions from the end of April to the end of June 1915. In this short period, Lloyd George as Liberal Chancellor of the Exchequer talked of the need for a man of 'push and go' to vitalise munitions supply; the press enthusiastically identified my grandfather as such a man; Kitchener took him from Armstrongs to head a War Office munitions committee; the Liberal government fell; Lloyd George, in the coalition that replaced it, became Minister of the newly set up Ministry of Munitions which absorbed the War Office committee; and, on 8 June, or thereabouts, he appointed my grandfather Director General of Munitions Supply.

In these few weeks the unanimous enthusiasm of the press, both London and provincial, and from *The Times* to *Titbits*, is extraordinary: 'Sir P. Girouard's New Post. Chosen as Chancellor's man of Push and Go.' 'His wide knowledge and wonderful business capacity.' 'One of the ablest organisers in service of the country.' 'Greatest railways engineer the army has ever produced.' 'A big man for a big job.' 'Sir Percy Girouard. Tributes to his organising genius.' 'Push and Go. Is Sir Percy Girouard the man?' 'There seems reason to congratulate the nation.' 'Nation's superman. Sir Percy Girouard the Chancellor's choice. His brilliant record.' 'Sir Percy Girouard – Hustler. Has the British Government finally found its man?' 'The Superman of Shells. Sir Percy Girouard's wonderful career.' And over and over again, in photographs or in drawings large and small, the public were regaled with my grandfather's face and monocle.

Tucked between the endpapers of the cuttings book is a copy of Lloyd George's bleak little letter of 22 July, giving him the sack. He explained why in a paragraph of his *War Memoirs*, published in 1933–36. It is a killer:

> I soon discovered that . . . his stock of vitality had been burnt out in great tasks driven through under tropical suns – the vivid spirit was still there and the habits and movement of an old energy were also visible, but these took the form of an unsettling restlessness rather than a steady activity. He dashed about from the War Office to the Ministry and back from the Ministry to the War Office, where he spent most of his time, to and from one department after another attending to no detail of any kind in any of them. When he came to see me he was always in such a hurry that he never sat down. He rushed into my room like a man who was chased by a

problem and could not stay too long lest it caught him up . . . All this feverish hustle gave the impression of a propelling eagerness to urge everybody along, but it was the symptom of a spent nervous system.

But even if this picture is exaggerated, or distorted (and I suspect it is), there were other reasons which made my grandfather's survival in the Ministry unlikely. It was Kitchener, not Lloyd George, who had brought him to London. He was, as Lloyd George put it, 'delivered over to me with the munition problem' from the War Office. He was an 'out-and-out Kitchener man', and Lloyd George wanted his own men, not Kitchener's, round him. He had been built up as a star; and there was only room for one star in the Ministry. The immediate cause of his dismissal came when Lloyd George was sent down by the Cabinet to Wales, to deal (as he successfully did) with a major coal-miners' strike. When he came back he discovered that my grandfather had arranged, in his absence and without telling him, to escort the King on a tour of munitions factories in the Midlands. Although Lloyd George had professed to be uninterested in royal occasions, he was furious. When my grandfather returned from the tour, he found the letter of dismissal on his desk. As Michael Smith writes in his biography of my grandfather:

> The long search for the 'Man of push and go' was finally over; he was revealed as Lloyd George himself and, as one press wag had it: 'When two men "push", one man usually "goes".'

Whatever the rights and wrongs of the story, my grandfather's dismissal by Lloyd George was an appalling blow to him. What should have been the culmination of his career proved a fiasco; his reputation, his pride and his self-confidence suffered. Moreover, it was only one of three blows, all equally devastating in different ways, which followed each other in succession: his divorce in 1914, his dismissal in 1915, my grandmother's death in 1916. I think (though the evidence is not certain) that it was now that he started on the really heavy drinking, which ended up in his becoming an alcoholic. Anyway, from now on his career did not collapse, but slowly, and by fits and starts, petered out.

At the enthusiastic invitation of the board, he returned to Armstrong Whitworths as managing director (the vice-chairmanship had been filled in his absence). He stayed in the firm for another seven years, during which he earned more than at any previous time in his career. But they were not years of much achievement. Armstrong's was engaged in what proved to be a losing fight with Vicker's, its great rival; perhaps my grandfather was no longer the man to lead and win this fight, but in 1920 he had the humiliation of being passed over for the chairmanship in favour of Sir Glyn West, who was ten years younger and had been his protégé. West in fact proved a disaster, an arrogant and self-deluding autocrat who led the firm to financial collapse and takeover by Vickers in 1927. My grandfather had no responsibility for this, never supported West's projects and left the firm in 1923. But he was now on the loose, drinking, and apparently a failure.

He was rescued by his niece, Virginia Skynner. She had come to England from her home town of Winnipeg as companion to a rich Winnipeg widow, and stayed on to keep house for her uncle. She was aged 25, he 56. He had been invited by a cement manufacturer, William Roberts, to help him set up a new cement works at Holborough, in Kent. I don't suppose Virginia had anything to do with this, but she certainly helped him to make the project a success. She looked after him, got him off the bottle, and gave him love and support (my father did not know of the letters he wrote her, did not realise how much she came to mean to him, and did not like her). For four years they lived quietly at Holborough Cottage, next to the cement company's offices at Holborough Court. The business was tiny compared to Armstrong's, but the work interested him, and the company did well. They were years that both of them looked back to with nostalgia.

At the end of 1927 there was a boardroom coup, Roberts ceased to be chairman, and my grandfather left the company with him. This was not necessarily a disaster; he had capital and experience, and invested both in starting up a new cement works at Askeham, not far away from Holborough. It failed, however, and he lost all his money.

He did not give up. He was no longer able to provide a home for Virginia, but he set to work to re-establish his fortunes. When the surviving letters to Virginia start in February 1930 (hers to him have been lost), she had gone back to her family in Winnipeg, and he was about to leave London and go to Colombia, sent out by an Anglo-Belgian firm of cement manufacturers to report on prospects of starting up works there. The thought of going on his travels again exhilarated him. He would 'spread sails on the new Odyssey' (he had been reading Tennyson's *Ulysses*, I suspect), '. . . though 63 is late.' Meanwhile, 'Keep the head high old girl,' and 'How can one be serious or sentimental with such a pen and such ink.'

He went on two trips to Colombia, one of four and one of eight months, looking into the prospects for gold as well as cement, indefatigably travelling long distances, by rail, river or air, undergoing great differences of altitude and climate, and full of hope. He sent back detailed reports, which were received with enthusiasm by his sponsors. 'Not bad for an old buffer after all sweetheart. The reports *are* excellent, if I say so, and they haven't had my best as yet. I like the country, its people and its problems and I haven't been in better fettle for years, it is like the best of my African days.' He wrote her long and lively letters, full of news and optimism, but always saying how much he missed her, and thought of her: 'I miss miss miss miss you . . . I miss you always and ever . . . In walking last night the stars were bright and the full moon here, I thought if you looked south and I north we would see the same old stars and moon.' On his second trip he had two months' serious illness, but recovered and 'my darling girl, your last letter was one of the sweetest I have had in my life, and you cannot know how it comforted me and how much I want our lives to join up again and they will. I miss you more than I can say . . . it will be a joyous day when I can cable for you once more to join me, never to leave me again.'

That day never came. What he found waiting for him on his return was the London of the slump, where 'even gold-mines in Colombia are seemingly dross'. He worked away, and tried to encourage Virginia, 'Darling be brave and patient, things are coming right,' but they did not come right. For fifteen months he was on his own in London watching his prospects fade. His consolations were my sister, whom he adored, and our mother, who gave him a friendship that meant much to him. 'I felt I was sliding away,' he wrote after an illness, 'and the one hand really stretched out to me was Blanchie's.' But, as he wrote to Virginia, 'I only want you really.' He was old, tired, sick, poor and lonely, but he sent her what little news he had, and tried to keep up their spirits. On 19 September 1932, he wrote, 'Please do not get down-hearted even though affairs do not appear rosy, there is I believe a silver lining to this dark cloud. We must both grin and bear existing conditions, however trying . . . Goodby my dearest, I miss you more than ever.' A few days later he was taken ill, and he died on 26 September 1932, aged 65.

I first read these letters in, I think, 1997, when I was much the same age as my grandfather had been at the time he wrote them, and going through a period of great unhappiness. They knocked me out.

Virginia lived on in Winnipeg until 1981. She never married, and when she died her body was carried across the Atlantic and buried in the plot next to my grandfather's grave in Brookwood Cemetery. Their two gravestones are side by side – his large and rather beautifully lettered and carved, hers one-third the size, a rather sad little slab, inscribed in meagre commercial lettering to 'Virginia Cranwill Skynner, loving and beloved niece of Colonel Sir Percy Girouard.'

My grandmother had been buried in the graveyard by the church in Budleigh Salterton, and a memorial tablet was put up to her in the church. I think only one bomb fell on Budleigh Salterton during the last war, but it landed on the church. My sister and I went to see this with our father on 18 September 1943, when we were on holiday there together. The church had been restored, but as I wrote in an unformed script in my diary: 'We have found the memorial to daddy's mother, lying on a rubbish heap. It is very sad.'

I don't think our father made any attempt to have the memorial pieced together again. It was perhaps too badly broken, and anyway he was quite unsentimental about graves and memorials. He was equally unsentimental about places, with one exception: he had strong feelings about Budleigh Salterton. I don't know whether this was just because he had had happy holidays there as a boy, as he certainly had in the years when my great-grandmother was living there; or, more specifically, because he had been happy there for a few weeks with his mother, just before she died (she died when he was away at school, as I was when my mother was killed). Anyway, he always loved going back there, and the few days that I spent there with him in 1987 was the last really happy time that we had together, before old age closed over him.

15

Aunt Evie

WHEN MY MOTHER was killed in a car crash in October 1940, the future of her three children – my sister Teresa aged twelve, myself aged nine, and my sister Mary aged two – was a problem. Our house in London was shut down; my father was in the army and moving around; we could have gone to our grandmother or aunts in Ireland, but that would have meant going to school there, and communication between the two countries in the war was not easy, and was sometimes dangerous. But difficulties were solved when my great-aunt Evie offered to have us come to live with her in Derbyshire.

I will always be grateful to her for taking us in, and giving us a secure and stable background for the next three years. Admittedly she was in a position to do so without too much inconvenience to herself, and she had been very fond of my mother, her sister's child. Even so, for a 70-year-old widow, already supplied with seven children and 22 grandchildren of her own, and having recently removed into what was for her a small house, to take on three small nephews and nieces along with their Swiss governess was a kind and generous act.

We had, in the past, stayed with her at both Hardwick and Chatsworth, as well as going to parties at her house overlooking the Mall in Carlton Gardens, from which I well remember, though a very small child, watching the processions for both George V's golden jubilee and his funeral. But at that age the foreground was filled with nannies and servants; 'grown-ups' were insubstantial figures beyond them. It was only when we first went to Derbyshire, early in 1941, that she came into focus.

She took us in without any obvious display of warmth or affection for us as motherless children. She never hugged me or, as far as I can remember, even kissed me; that was not her way, or indeed the way of most women of her age and background. For much of the day we did not see her. But she was always kind, and always interested in what we were doing. I have nothing but good memories of her. According to some of her children and grandchildren, although good to them when they were small, she could be difficult and censorious when they were growing up, but that was never my own experience.

I have a favourite photograph of her, taken by my sister on one of the loggias at Hardwick in 1955. It brings her back vividly to me. She is seated straight-backed on a folding wooden chair; I cannot imagine her ever reclining in a deckchair. She wears, as she habitually did, a suit of jacket and skirt, the jacket open to show a frilled white shirt-front; thick stockings and sensible brogues with low heels; one of those round felt hats with a brim, not unlike a trilby, worn by old ladies of her generation, from under which protrudes her hair, grown long, but in the daytime put up and carefully curled. She is nice-looking, with a slightly beaky nose; she was never pretty, unlike her sister, my grandmother, who as a young woman was ravishingly so. She looks exactly what she was: a well-cared-for old lady of the upper classes, but a friendly and approachable one; even so, not someone with whom one could take liberties.

In the war years, once a week or so, this light-grey outfit was translated, hat and all, into one of navy-blue with red facings, and she went off to officiate in her almost inevitable role as President of the Derbyshire Red Cross.

Her voice was not at all loud, rather slow, and exquisitely articulated – quite unlike the rapid, swooping, slurred speech of her Cecil daughter-in-law. Her one peculiarity of pronunciation that I can remember was that she pronounced 'great' as 'grey'. She walked slowly and deliberately: I never saw her hurrying or shouting, or in a rage, or helpless with laughter; but she was by no means without humour. She once told my sister that it was a sin to be shy; I think she had suffered from shyness as a young woman, but had learned to overcome it.

Lansdowne House, her home as a child when in London, backed on to Devonshire House, but was separated from it by a narrow alleyway; she described to me how this was crossed by a little footbridge, so that the children of the two families could run to and fro into each other's gardens. So when she married Victor Cavendish in 1892 she was, in effect, marrying the boy next door. They lived at Holker Hall in Lancashire and in one of the bow-fronted houses on Park Lane, until in 1908 he inherited from his uncle as Duke of Devonshire. For the next thirty years, with a break when her husband served as Governor-General of Canada, her life was structured by an ordered progress between four or five country houses in England and Ireland, and a big house in London. Of these, Chatsworth was the grandest, but Hardwick the one she loved most. Her husband had a stroke in 1925, and survived it incapacitated but with a filthy temper, leaving her as effectively the head of the family; but when he died in 1938 she cannot have grieved much, or regretted the prospect of life without him, with Hardwick as her dower house, a house on Eaton Square and an ample income. But the outbreak of war in 1939 changed all that: Hardwick was closed, the London house given up, and she moved into Edensor House, on the edge of the park at Chatsworth. Her son and daughter-in-law, who had only recently moved into

Chatsworth, left it for Churchdale Hall, a modest country house five miles away. Debo Cavendish, newly married to their second son Andrew, moved into a house nearby. Chatsworth was taken over by Penrhos College, a girls' school evacuated from Colwyn Bay in North Wales, and rows of little iron beds filled the state rooms.

Edensor House had the size and style of a large rectory: two storeys only, vaguely classical, a bay window on the garden side, a big cedar tree in the garden, a service wing to one side, a wide entrance hall, a roomy staircase, two living or drawing rooms and a dining room, good-sized rooms but not at all grand in themselves, though furnished rather grandly from Chatsworth (hall furniture by William Kent, and so on). The household staff in this cut-down establishment seems lavish enough today. I think we just overlapped with the footman and chauffeur, before they went off to join the armed forces. The household was left with butler, doubling up as occasional chauffeur, cook, kitchen maid, housekeeper, housemaid, my Aunt Evie's own lady's maid, and our governess. There was also a gardener, who was exempted from call-up because he had weak lungs.

Frances, the housemaid, was young and pretty; she was related to Olive, who ran the telephone exchange in the porter's lodge at Chatsworth, and as a treat used to let us plug and unplug the leads with their long tubes. Enid, the kitchen maid, was more soulful, and was learning the violin; her family lived in the farm that one passed walking along the edge of Chatsworth Park to Baslow. Of May, the housekeeper, I have little recollection. Mrs Mellor, the cook, was grumpy and did not like little boys, so I seldom if ever went into the kitchen; she was a very good cook, though. To the butler's pantry I had free access; I would sit up at the table while Ilott, the butler (*Mister* Ilott, to me), polished the silver

and talked to me, rather surprisingly considering his exceed-
ingly butler-like appearance, about the uselessness of the
upper classes and the sterling qualities of the British working-
man.

He was not a warm person, unlike Miss Webb, Aunt Evie's
lady's maid, soon known to us as 'Webbie'. She was fattish, a
little blowsy, and had a ribald sense of humour. She and Aunt
Evie complained about each other, spoke their minds to each
other, and were devoted to each other. The most prominent
features in her room, as in the rooms of all ladies' maids at the
time, were a sewing machine and a tailor's dummy. It had a
distinctively warm, sweet, cloying atmosphere, the combination, perhaps, of women's underwear and of the windows
never being opened. It was a comforting place, where we were
always welcome; she was the nearest to a maternal figure in
our lives.

The house reflected, in fact, in reduced form the life which
Aunt Evie had always led. Its ceremonial and practical pivot
was the audience which she gave in bed around nine o'clock
every morning as, I imagine, she had been doing for forty
years or more. The cook, the housekeeper, any family or
guests who were staying, and we children assembled on the
staircase landing outside the door of her bedroom. This was a
large and pleasant room with a bay window, above the main
drawing room. Aunt Evie would be sitting upright in bed,
with her breakfast tray in front of her, wearing a lace bed-
jacket and lace cap, with her hair already done for the day
and Webbie in attendance. In turn cook, housekeeper, house
guests and children were admitted to wish her a good
morning and discuss the activities of the day.

We always had lunch with her, unless she was away; when
we were older we started to come down to dinner as well. The
food at Edensor was distinctive. In her position, and in the
middle of the Chatsworth estate, it is hard to believe that she

could not have eased our diet. But she kept rigidly to wartime rations. At the dining room table each of us, she included, had our personal weekly allowance of sugar and butter set out at our places in our own glass jars and china pots; it was up to us to make it last out the week or, if not, to go without until the next allotment arrived. The war situation appealed to frugality and love of experiment, both elements in her character. At Chatsworth in her reign guests were sometimes disconcerted by being served with dishes such as lambs' tails as the main course. This just seemed eccentric; but in wartime she had every excuse for looking for unexpected foods, ways to use leftovers, and vegetable replacements for meat or fish. So she enjoyed herself, and Mrs Mellor could translate her ideas into eatable form.

She put on her gardening gloves, and picked the nettles (only young ones) herself for soup and as a replacement for spinach, and the camomile for camomile tea. At lunch, favourite main dishes were something called carroty oats, a kind of mixture of porridge and carrots, and beetroot cream, a combination of beetroot and flour. We ate a great deal of home-made brawn. Another favourite was a grey sloppy mess called barm – a by-product of the brewing process. This was for medicine not meals; it was said to be good for one. We were regularly dosed with it, and so was Eric, the weak-lunged gardener. I don't recollect the dish made from used barley-corn after barley-water had been extracted from it, as described by her grand-daughter-in-law Debo. But I loved Edensor food, carroty oats and brawn especially, and have made useless and disastrous attempts to recreate the former.

Somewhere in the woods at Chatsworth she had stocked up a shed or cottage with provisions. We were to retreat there if the Germans came. I never went there, or even discovered where it was, but found the concept of it deeply romantic. Another unexpected contribution to the war effort was her white goat. I'm not sure what its contribution was: not milk or cheese, I am pretty sure; perhaps it was thought to replace a lawnmower. She used to take it for walks, on a long chain. She was old and not very strong, the goat was young and lusty, and she was hauled helplessly across the tussocks and furrows of the park by this impetuous animal. One summer holiday, Teresa and I were given the care of a small and rather unlovable pony. I have a vivid memory of the servants and children grouped outside the garden door; Ilott holding the pony; the door opening and Aunt Evie emerging wearing black silk knickers tucked into her stockings and a macintosh; and Ilott helping her to mount the pony. The image seems so unlikely that I had sometimes wondered if it was a dream, until I came across a reference to it in a letter written by me at the time to my sister.

We were not cosseted. My minute bedroom had just about enough room for a bed and a framed photograph of Queen Alexandra, fenced in with diamonds; I had to make the bed myself. When Aunt Evie was away, we were sent to eat in the servants' hall. She set me to weeding in the garden, and paid me sixpence an hour; the accumulated total was paid before I went back to school at the end of the holidays. She was conscientious in seeing that we went to our Catholic church on Sundays, walking on our own the three miles over the hill to the little tin chapel at Bakewell, or the similar distance across the fields to the grander church at Hassop. Otherwise, we comparatively seldom got away from Edensor and Chatsworth. Two or three times a year, especially at Christmas, we went to lunch or tea at Churchdale, where Elizabeth and Anne Cavendish were older than us, and seemed impressively sophisticated; they were friendly, though, took us on a tour, and showed us their two cows, named after their grandmothers, Evie and Alice. Every now and then, Debo Cavendish came cantering up the drive in her pony cart, a very glamorous sight. But much of the time we just roamed on our own, through the empty park, pleasure grounds and woods at Chatsworth.

I was amused, years later, to come across Consuelo Vanderbilt's description of staying, as a girl, at Government House in Calcutta when Lord Lansdowne was Viceroy, and being appalled at how badly educated his daughter Beatrice, my grandmother, was. Aunt Evie, her elder sister, was no better: both girls were governess-educated, which meant barely educated at all. She was well aware of this in late life, and deplored it, but lacked the technique and perhaps the time to educate herself; she had a great deal of curiosity, but no method.

She was not a great reader. Although the massive catalogues of the Royal Drawings, inscribed and sent to her at regular intervals by Queen Mary, whose Mistress of the Robes she was, were prominent on the shelves, I don't remember her ever looking at them. But from living with and having to look after valuable things she had acquired a good deal of knowledge of them, and a feeling for their arrangement. What she chose for Edensor showed her discrimination. I have a vivid memory of its rooms, and am intrigued when, at Chatsworth or Hardwick, I come across pieces or pictures that I knew there. What I have never seen again is the big old dolls' house, containing much furniture of the same date, that we had in our nursery or schoolroom.

She was fascinated by natural history; if she had lived into the television age she would have adored David Attenborough's programmes. The only book I recollect her reading with enthusiasm was one on the animal life of tropical Africa. She lent it to me, and we had enjoyable talks about the habits of hyaenas and flying foxes. She was always interested in my own enthusiasms – first wildflowers, then prehistoric man, only at the end architecture – and we had discussions about these too. I was a serious little boy.

She had theories about things and people. Something about the way in which my little sister used her thumb convinced her that she was going to grow up to be a sculptor. Something else she did – I don't know what – convinced her that she was, aged three or four, on the road to sexual depravity; my father got a long letter on the subject. My elder sister and I were very close and did everything together. Once, before one or other of us went off to school, we spent the night in the same bed together, talking deep into the night, as a treat for ourselves. It was quite innocent, but evoked another immensely long letter for my poor father. She once told me how, when Devonshire House had been sold, she and her husband thought that they might make Chiswick House, which belonged to them, their London home. They went down to look at it, and then took a row on the Thames, lost their oars, and were carried adrift down the river. Aunt Evie envisaged her daughters going rowing with young men, and being caught in compromising situations, and the idea of Chiswick was given up. She had had her own admirer, Lord Bicester; the Chinese dragons and little Chinese trees with delicate jade leaves that he had given her were prominently displayed in the drawing rooms at Edensor; but I have no reason to suppose he was more than an admirer. Sex was dangerous, perhaps also fascinating, but one did not talk about it. Perhaps, like many respectable ladies, she was curious about the lives of those less respectable. The nearest she ever came to sexual innuendo with me was at the time of my father's disastrously short second marriage. I had come down from school for the wedding, and by the time I returned for the holidays the marriage was over. Aunt Evie talked to me about it, and said in her precise hesitating voice – 'I believe she is rather – rather – masculine.' I told my father this years later, and he was touched by what he saw as her loyalty to him in what had been a distressing episode.

She did not reminisce much about the past, and I did not question her about it. Only a few scraps have stuck in my memory. As a little girl she was sent to take soup to the deserving poor, but did not enjoy it, as poor people seemed to her like a different race, so small and misshapen. She was taught deportment and dancing by Madame Taglioni who, as I later learnt, had been perhaps the greatest dancer of her day, had made her debut in 1822, but in old age gave classes to little boys and girls in London.

She told me of the inkstand that Gladstone had given as a wedding present, and of how she had given this, in turn, to her son-in-law Harold Macmillan when he became Foreign Secretary, to have on his writing table in the Foreign Office, from which, to her distress, it was later stolen. She said that she was always grateful to him 'because he had behaved so well over Dorothy'. At the time I did not understand what this was about. She had a good description of Blanche Curzon, Lord Curzon's unmarried sister, showing her the monuments in the church at Kedleston: 'All Curzons, Duchess. No Tom, Dick or Harry here.'

Some of these scraps may date from visits to Hardwick, not Edensor. Towards the end of 1943, as transport got easier, we began to holiday in other places, but still with Edensor as our base up to spring 1944. (When I came back from a visit to a godmother and her husband, she asked me what they were like and said, 'I believe they are very smart.' Being 'smart' epitomised everything that she most disliked.) I went over to Hardwick for the first time since before the war in April 1944, and reported to my father, 'It is beautifully tidy inside and there are not many dust sheets around, and [it] is ready to be moved into at any moment, if Aunt Evie's ever able to.' But she was still at Edensor in January 1946 when I stayed there and she took me to see Heathy Lea, a house on the edge of the moor above Chatsworth where the 6th or Bachelor Duke had kept his mistress, and which she was thinking of moving into as an alternative to Hardwick. Hardwick won, however, and she finally went back there later in 1946, I think, or some time in 1947. I went to stay regularly for the next ten years; I was always welcome to invite myself, and to bring a friend if I wanted.

In one of the very few letters from her that I still have, written in June 1949, she wrote, 'We always seem to be very busy but never catch up, either in the house or garden. The whole population is getting old and there is nobody young to replace them. The house men don't see the moth and the garden men don't notice the weeds, so I spend my time hunting them round.' She lived at Hardwick with none of the grandeur of pre-war days. Her own quarters were contracted into the southern end of the house; she gave up the big dining room in the former Low Great Chamber, and all except one of the bedrooms in the northern half, including the nurseries, now abandoned and empty except for a set of engravings of the eruption of Vesuvius, which I remembered vividly from my childhood. But she still occupied, as she always had, what had been Bess of Hardwick's own rooms: her big withdrawing room on the first floor, her bedchamber beyond it, and the charming small room beyond that in the southern tower, looking down the long yew-walk of the garden. This became Aunt Evie's own sitting room or boudoir. Bess of Hardwick had died in the bedchamber, beneath its great two-storey chimneypiece framed with busty caryatids; so had the Bachelor Duke, who had loved Hardwick and done much for it. Aunt Evie must have hoped to die there too.

In terms of her own rooms (the state rooms had their own cleaners), she was left with much the same accommodation as at Edensor but with rather fewer servants to run them. But the personnel had changed. Webbie was still there of course, her sewing machine and tailor's dummy now set up beneath another great chimneypiece, with huge talbots supporting the Shrewsbury coat of arms, next to Aunt Evie's bedroom. The morning audiences continued, exactly as at Edensor. But the housekeeper was now Mrs Frost, a woman of character, with a clever son at university. The cook was Mrs Phillips, a nicer woman but a worse cook than Mrs Mellor. The butler, Tagg, was similarly a much nicer man than Ilott, but by no means a professional butler. He was a former coal-miner, who laid the table by guesswork, putting out far more than the necessary amount of cutlery, to make sure.

Meals were served in a small, rather boring, dining room on the ground floor. Aunt Evie never came down to breakfast. At lunch and dinner Tagg passed the food round, holding the dishes in a very unbutlerlike way, and in the intervals stood behind Aunt Evie's chair, filling her glass from time to time from a carafe of what appeared to be water, but was in fact neat gin. If there were visitors tea was occasionally served in the Great Hall, as it had been before the war. On days when the house was open to the public, Aunt Evie, along with anyone staying in the house, invariably went to have tea alongside the tourists in the Elizabethan kitchen, now used as a refreshment room. She was always pleased if people came up and talked to her. After dinner we would go up for coffee to her little sitting room in the south turret. One wall of this was filled with a great Elizabethan embroidery, framed and glazed; and it was pleasant to sit there talking as the light changed to twilight. One evening I sat on reading after she had gone to bed. The room had two doors, one opening directly into her bedroom; this opened suddenly, and she was standing there, in a nightdress to the ground, her long hair let down and her teeth out; she mouthed a little, and then the door shut. She did not allude to this incident the next morning.

In conversation one never quite knew what she would come up with. She would wonder, perhaps, whether a miniature vacuum cleaner could be invented, to extract woodworm from furniture; her previous technique had been a little hammer, with which she would rap the relevant piece to give the worms concussion. On another visit she produced a theory that manure from the sewage farms should be carted on to the slag-heaps which were all round Hardwick, which should then be planted with pink carnations.

Such remarks only occasionally came to the surface. It would be a mistake to think of her as eccentric; but she had an active mind, which sometimes moved in unexpected channels. On the whole, my visits were uneventful; often I was the only person there, for she lived very quietly. I spent long hours just wandering round the house on my own. I walked slowly with her through the gardens, one of the three or four gardens I like best in the world, its formal early Victorian layout softened by Aunt Evie's Gertrude-Jekyll-style alterations, which had replaced little flower beds with open lawn, and bedding out with herbaceous borders; and deliciously divided by its clipped hedges into four main segments, two for a kitchen garden mixed with flowers, one for an orchard, one lawn and cedar trees. Or I would have enjoyable gossips with Webbie. She could do a brilliant imitation of Aunt Evie talking about her: 'Poor Webb, of course she's beginning to go a little . . .' etc.

But, quiet though they were, I remember my visits with great pleasure, above all because just being at Hardwick, walking all round it, through its huge empty rooms and up on to the roof, was such a delight; but also because I was fond of Aunt Evie, and Webbie too, and they, I think, were fond of me.

The fact that I responded strongly to Hardwick was a link between us. Even before her widowhood, when she spent at

most a month or two a year there, it had always been her
favourite of the many Cavendish houses. I am not really qualified to talk about her time at Chatsworth. I think that she
never quite came to terms with it. Its enormous scale may not
have been to her taste, and she certainly much disliked
Wyatville and neo-classical sculpture. She (I say 'she' because
I think she was more interested in architecture and decoration
than her husband) did some good things there – in terms of
conservation, getting the fading Old Master drawings off the
walls and into folders; in terms of display, installing
Romaine-Walker's grand staircase and balconies in the
Painted Hall. Elsewhere she was responsible for rather too
much dun or cream paint, since repainted, and the removal of
bits of Wyatville, since replaced. The great disaster of her time
was the destruction of Paxton's Great Stove or Conservatory
in 1920, a decision taken at long distance after wartime
neglect and during the Duke's term as Governor General in
Canada. In after-life she regretted the destruction; she had
become interested in Paxton, whose granddaughter Violet
Markham (Mrs Carruthers in my time) was her greatest
friend. She never talked to me about the demolition of Devonshire House, and I don't know what she felt about it, or
whether she had anything to do with the careful storage of all
its fittings at Chatsworth, from which they emerged so
surprisingly for the recent sale. I like the story of her realising
that the junior servants at Chatsworth had never even seen
the state rooms there, and assembling them to take them
round herself.

But it was Hardwick that she loved. She had first come
there before her husband inherited, when it was lent every
summer to Lady Blanche Egerton, the sister of the 8th Duke.
In her notes on Hardwick she describes how Lady Blanche
'used to sit in the morning in the gallery making sketches and
notes – the sun streaming on to her white hair and widow's

cap – and she loved to talk about what she hoped we should do when we in our turn should have the care of the place. I think she left a benign and friendly atmosphere.'

Blanche Egerton died in 1907, and Aunt Evie took on the care of Hardwick when her husband inherited in 1908. From then on work at Hardwick was fairly continuous, though all of a very conservative nature. The exterior stonework was restored according to the best SPAB principles of the day – in the long term disastrous, as it turned out, but a bonus was that Basil Stallybrass, the architect involved, went on to publish a long pioneering article on Bess of Hardwick's building accounts. An experiment in retouching the faded paint-work of the frieze in the High Great Chamber was fortunately abandoned, and it was left faded. The house was floored throughout with rush matting, a traditional local product; the smell of it in other houses always makes me think of Hardwick. Electricity was introduced in most of the rooms; the one surviving old leaded lantern was fitted for electric light and copied for use elsewhere in the house. A hotplate was installed outside the Low Great Chamber, discreetly hidden in a sixteenth-century chest.

Aunt Evie was proud of the lime avenue that she planted in 1920, running away from the east facade of the house on a wine-glass plan that made it seem larger than it was; she had been similarly proud, she told me, of the apse that increased the apparent length of the church near Holker, which she and her husband built in their early married years.

But it was the textiles at Hardwick which inspired her especial devotion. The house was filled to overflowing with them, both tapestries and embroideries, more so than any other house in Europe. From the later seventeenth century onwards, tapestry had been used like wallpaper, and any hangings not currently in use had been remorselessly cut up to fill gaps. One of her delights was to assemble such bits and pieces, stitch them together, and recreate the original whole. The most exciting re-assembly was undoubtedly that of the long strips of fifteenth-century tapestry that had been used to fill gaps between the windows in the Long Gallery. Joined together these resulted in the famous Hunting Tapestries, three huge scenes of medieval hunting, which had to be taken off to Chatsworth to show them, because there was no place at Hardwick; they are now in the Victoria & Albert Museum. Less ambitious rejoinings are still at Hardwick, including one piece of verdure tapestry stitched together by Aunt Evie and her daughter Maud out of 25 fragments, with a missing border and a few gaps replaced by the relevant design painted on canvas.

She did a great deal of straightforward repairs to tapestries as well, working on her own, or with an assistant, often one of her daughters. The attractive portrait and good likeness of her by Edward Halliday shows her doing this in the High Great Chamber; this, I think, is artistic licence, as is the dramatic streak of sunlight coming through an uncurtained window on to a tapestry, something that she would have never allowed. Her favourite place was at a big table set up in the tower bay letting off the Low Great Chamber, where she said that the light was best, and it is here that I remember her at work.

The embroideries at Hardwick are even more remarkable than the tapestries, and she was much concerned with them too, though I am not sure whether she ever worked on repairing them herself; perhaps she doubted her competence for this more delicate work. The repairs inaugurated by her on the great embroidery panels of Heroines, Virtues and Vices were carried out by two members of the Decorative Needlework Society, prior to their being put under glass. Some of their methods are criticised today, but the hanging were saved from the condition described by Aunt Evie, unprotected in the draughty hall, with bits falling off when the front door was opened. She continued the work inaugurated by the Bachelor Duke, of taking panels that had originally been cushion covers or table carpets, and mounting, framing and glazing them; the resulting silent assembly of allegorical or mythical figures and scenes, hanging on the walls or framed on screens, enormously enriches the house. She embroidered herself, working, I think, always with traditional patterns, on chair covers or firescreens. I recollect her at work on a firescreen that copied an embroidered panel framing the initials ES, for Elizabeth Shrewsbury; she copied it exactly except that ES was replaced by ED. She must have liked establishing herself as a successor to Bess of Hardwick in this way.

Her most ambitious venture with the embroideries was to bring back from Chatsworth the great state canopy that had been set up in the High Great Chamber for the 2nd Earl of Devonshire and his countess. She used it as the canopy for a new state bed in the former withdrawing chamber, and incorporated more embroideries of the period in its back-board and counterpane. The result was very splendid, but was dismantled in about 1990, and the canopy set up again in the High Great Chamber. Aunt Evie always said that making it into a bed had been one of her mistakes, but this was more because it was inconveniently enormous than because she had changed her mind about the idea. There was no function for a state canopy at Hardwick in the 1920s, but there was one for a state bed, in which George V and Queen Mary could be accommodated, and her great bed was devised accordingly.

She was the last person to live in the whole of Hardwick, and to occupy it as a country house rather than to preserve it as a monument, though I am sure that she felt she was doing both. Hardwick was furnished by her for large house parties, filling the whole house and occupying all the bedrooms; I remember once going in to see my mother as she breakfasted in bed beneath the canopy of one of the great four-posters. Only the High Great Chamber and Long Gallery were for looking and marvelling at rather than for use. The rooms were arranged according to the way in which they would be used, and in the taste of the 1890s, when hers had been formed: a love of textiles of all kinds, a preference for soft, faded colours, and a sensitively eclectic mixture of contents and patterns. Hardwick, unlike Chatsworth, gave her scope for this. Inevitably the Elizabethan elements predominated, though less so in the rooms most in use, especially the drawing room and dining rooms, which are still much as she left them. The dining room, quietly arranged with mostly eighteenth-century furnishings and portraits, struck a blow against Wyatville and neo-classicism: as she put it, it was 'a more effective setting for plate and pretty clothes than the over-decorated dining room at Chatsworth'.

The house party that I recollect seeing from a nursery angle as a child must have been one of the last to be held at Hardwick. When I came back in the 1950s there was no thought of the state bed ever being used again. Under the bed-cover it was lined with layers of lining paper or newspaper, as we found out when in my Oxford days an Austrian friend hurled himself through the curtains and sprawled on the bed, to a loud crackle of paper and the horror of a nearby cleaner.

Aunt Evie enjoyed talking with him, as she did with all my friends; she always liked meeting new people. On her own with me, she remarked that he was the 'perfect Arab type' and questioned me about his ancestry: 'Of course those continental families don't feel so deeply about the colour bar as we do.' She expressed interest when he told her that black women made good lovers, and analysed her daughters to see if they showed signs of negro blood: 'It's the long thigh that shows it up, my Maudie's got it, her Lascelles blood of course' (the Lascelles had made their money as Jamaican sugar planters).

Mostly, however, I came to Hardwick on my own. My visits acquired a new and exciting purpose when I started work on my PhD thesis on Robert Smythson in 1955. My choice of subject was almost inevitable, given the interest in Elizabethan architecture that Hardwick had given me, my own connection with it, and Smythson's likely contribution to its design. Aunt Evie was delighted and interested, and gave me all the help she could. She lent me her copy of Bess of Hardwick's long and detailed Probate Inventory, which she had carefully copied out by hand – I think the only copy before it was edited, printed and published in 1971. I had the use, too, of a long tour of Hardwick; also a manuscript which she had written in 1946 describing it room by room in the manner of the similar tour written by the 6th Duke. Above all, she arranged for Bess of Hardwick's account books to be brought back for my use to the muniment room at Hardwick, from which they had been removed to Chatsworth a decade or so previously. I worked on these in the muniment room, or sat in the drawing room or out in the loggia writing parts of my thesis.

My first publication, an article on aspects of Longleat, came out in *Country Life* in September 1956, and drew an immediate and long letter from her. 'I was thrilled to see your name over an article on Longleat in Country Life. I did not know you had been there or were working at its history . . . If Smythson had a hand in both houses, what more natural than that their owners employed some of the same craftsmen . . . The two families were intimate in Q. Eliz's days, and good

friends until this generation, but not much in common now!'
Webbie wrote too: 'What a splendid article you wrote about
Longleat. I was thrilled when I read it . . . Now then buck up,
I always said you were clever and would do things when you
grew up.'

In her letter Webbie told me that they were moving down
to the flat in London in October. In the early days after her
husband inherited Aunt Evie and her family seem occasionally to have spent Christmas at Hardwick, but heating the
house was barely feasible, and after her post-war return she
never did so. For a time she had a small and charming early
eighteenth-century house, with panelled interiors, in Smith
Square, Westminster, but as she got older she moved to the
greater convenience of a flat on an upper floor in York House,
off Kensington Church Street. This was furnished with her
own personal belongings, and was in no way remarkable; it
was like a lot of other pleasant flats of old ladies.

The unexpected death of her son Eddie in 1950 set in
motion the negotiations that ended with the transference of
Hardwick to the National Trust in 1956. I don't remember
her ever talking to me about this. Although she had the right
to continue living there she cannot have liked the feeling that
the house was not hers, and I have the impression that she
went there increasingly seldom up till her death in 1960. I
don't know when she last went, nor when I did, for that
matter – perhaps in 1958. I am sad that she did not live to see
my book on Robert Smythson or my edition of his drawings,
and I cannot remember ever showing her a copy of my thesis.

For a time her grandson John Stuart lodged with her in
London. He was her favourite grandchild, and she left him
most of what money of her own she had. They teased each
other, and got on very well together; he knew her much better
than I did. He had a good description of them sitting at meals
together, he opening his letters, she craning her rather long

neck to try and see who they were from. Webbie told him with much amusement of an incident when they were walking in Kensington Gardens together. Aunt Evie was very silent and Webbie asked her: 'What are you thinking about, Your Grace?' 'Sex, Webbie, I never think about anything else.'

I went to see her in York House shortly before she died. She was in bed and very feeble. She said, 'I suppose I am saying goodbye', but it was in no way an emotional meeting, nor would she have wanted it to be.